# LOUDIE

## The Story of the Girl from Arp, Texas

### ·A MEMOIR·

## LOUISE H. ORNELAS

Produced with the assistance of Fluency Organization, Inc.

Graphic design: Inkwell Creative

Printed in the U.S.A.

*To all my grandchildren and great grandchildren.*
*I love you and I want Jesus to be your best Friend.*

GRAN GRAN

# Table of Contents

## CHAPTER ONE

# Mother and Daddy

My mother was an angel. And my daddy was a toot. He really was. A wonderful toot. I worshipped both of my parents, but especially my daddy.

Daddy drank a lot, not a little. His friends would bring him home after a night at the bar and set him on the porch for me to take care of him. I wanted to be a nurse when I was younger, and caring for people came naturally to me even as a child. Quietly so no one could hear us, I would wipe his brow with a cool rag while he slept off the effects of the alcohol. He and I developed a special bond this way.

Daddy changed later in life in more ways than one. First, my dad was a lifelong Democrat until the landslide victory over the Democrats by the Republican candidate for president, Dwight D. Eisenhower, in 1952. Then he sang Eisenhower's praises the whole time he was in the White House to anyone who would listen. In my house hangs a portrait of Eisenhower that reminds me of Daddy. The second, but most important, transformation in Daddy's life from Mother's perspective was when Daddy came to know the Lord. Daddy had never in his life gone to church with Mother, but when he was saved he started taking her to Sunday school. My siblings and I could not believe it. Daddy even sat with Mother in her women's class, even though he was the only man there. Then they would go to the worship service together afterwards. He always had his Bible with him and busied himself reading it. Mother was always in a Bible study or at a church event. He offered to give the women in Mother's class rides to church if they were too ill to drive themselves, and he helped many of her friends with little things that needed doing around the house. He would always do anything he could for anyone without having to be asked.

My dad could fix most anything that needed fixing around our home, but the one thing he never did learn to do was tie a tie to wear to church. Fortunately, he didn't have to learn how because Mother always tied them for him. He would carefully loosen the knot while he was changing clothes after church then slip it off from around his weathered neck and hang it up in his closet until it was time to wear it again the next Sunday.

My siblings and I were all playmates because we were all born just two years apart, except for the last child. The oldest was born Emma Juanice, but she didn't like that name and as soon as she was old enough she changed it to Jean. Mother had Jean when she was just twenty years old. I was born next in line after Jean in 1925 in Las Cruces, New Mexico, when Mother was twenty-two. My parents lived for a while in New Mexico while Daddy worked at my aunt and uncle's fruit farm, but they eventually moved to Arp for good to raise the rest of their family. They named me Myrtle Louise Herrington. I went by my middle name, but some of my school friends called me Loudie. Many times I asked my mother why she named me Myrtle. She finally said it was one of her girlfriends' names and she had always loved it.

Al was next and the oldest boy. Although I loved all of my brothers in a special way, Charlie was my younger brother and was especially beautiful to me. Al served in World War II and Charlie served in the Air Force during the Korean War. Ellen and Ann were my younger sisters and Billy Creel was the baby of our large family. Jean, Charlie, and Ellen died many years ago. When I began writing this book about my memories, Al was still alive, but he died in June of 2017 after an illness. Now only Ann, Billy, and I are still living.

Mother and Daddy were busy raising seven children of their own when her sister (who lived across the highway from us in Arp) died of pneumonia. We took in her three sons to make their home with us without a second thought. They fit right into our family and we didn't think anything about the close quarters. Personally, I was glad to have the extra boys around because it meant that we always had a readymade softball team to play out in the backyard anytime we wanted!

As if our house wasn't already crowded enough with ten children, we sometimes snuck our pet goat, Patsy, past our parents so she could sleep with us on summer nights. We adored Patsy and when she stared at us with her beady little eyes she seemed to be saying she loved us, too! But when we accidently went outside and left her in the house one day, Patsy got so bored and hungry that she chewed the curtains right off the window in our room and we got in plenty of trouble. My parents ended up giving Patsy away to another family, but we were glad that they at least let us keep our one-legged chicken we called Betty Boop!

My family lived inside the city limits along the Arp highway between two oil refineries. It never got completely dark at our house because of two giant flares constantly burning against the night sky. We could play games in our backyard all evening when school was out and not have to turn in when it was dark like our other friends had to do. The orange glow against our faces and the night air made us feel as though we were getting away with something exciting.

Daddy worked as a spread man on a pipeline in the booming oil fields of East Texas when oil was as plentiful as iced tea in the South in summer. He also worked on the Big Inch, an emergency pipeline built during World War II that few people in our area knew about. The Big Inch stretched from East Texas to New Jersey and provided a safer route for delivering precious oil for the war effort after German submarines attacked our oil tankers in the Gulf. I was proud of my father and remember how his hands were permanently stained dark from his work in the oil fields.

The only problem was that oil wells were popping up all over Texas, and his job would sometimes take him away from us for a week or more. How we missed him when he was gone. Never one to avoid hard work, he made sure that he always left his children with plenty of jobs to do in his absence.

A farmer at heart, my father also somehow made time to grow several crops. My daddy seemed to have extraordinary luck with vegetables. He could stick small potato plants in the ground and tend to them until the dirt was covered in green bundles of potato leaves. You never saw so many potatoes in your life. He could do the same thing with tomatoes. People say I inherited my dad's green thumb, but last year my tomato plants grew six feet tall without a single tomato!

My mom was also a wonderful cook. It seems my mother was always opening our home to any friends or neighbors who wanted to come by for a visit. No matter how busy she was keeping house for ten children, Mother offered to feed her guests something she had baked herself. People knew they were sincerely welcome at her table.

I remember the peas and cornbread she could whip up at a moment's notice. She'd sometimes pick plump blackberries from our pasture to make blackberry pies from scratch. We also had a peach orchard and enjoyed fresh peach pie after dinner every summer. My favorite meal was on Sunday afternoons. We always had fried chicken on those days because we usually had guests over after church. My siblings and I sometimes complained among ourselves because we didn't get the pieces of chicken we wanted if the preacher visited because he always ate them! Sometimes when I take a deep breath I can still smell mother's yeast rolls. I'd often sneak one off her baking sheet and eat it absolutely raw before it even went in the oven. I still ask my favorite restaurant today to undercook their rolls for me. That way, no one else at the table eats them!

A typical day during my childhood started out like most any other day growing up in the Thirties. We all got busy doing chores and picking Daddy's tomatoes off the vines or picking whatever crops happened to be growing at the time. When we weren't doing chores, Daddy let us ride on the horse-drawn ground sled while he cut the bean poles. My siblings and I would always fight over who got to do the dishes after eating lunch at home because that lucky person would get to listen to *Stella Dallas* on the radio. This ongoing soap opera captivated me. It was the story of a mother named Stella Dallas who loses her daughter to a man of wealth and privilege. The writers kept us hanging in each episode with dramatic stories about their lives, and we could not wait to tune in the next day to find out what happened.

We did not consider ourselves poor, and if someone had asked, we would have said we were rich. We had all the food we could eat and never lacked for anything that we needed. Besides, everyone I knew in Arp was just like us, so we didn't think we were missing out. Arp sits along an East Texas railroad line and Texas Highway 135, just outside of Tyler, Texas, in Smith County. We rode the 18 miles between Tyler and Arp in our family's old wooden wagon whenever Mother needed to get fabric to make our clothes or Daddy needed some special supplies for working around the house or in the fields. We'd park in the lot with all the other wagons near the downtown square in Tyler, and my siblings and I would spend the day looking at everything there was to see in the big city.

Arp was originally just a little settlement in the 1800s

called Strawberry Junction. It was renamed "Arp" supposedly in part because it was a short and sweet name that was easy for strawberry farmers to stencil on their crates. But more people know it as the last name of a journalist who went by the pen name William Arp. It was not a popular place to live at first and served mainly as a hub for farmers to sell their goods. But when oil was discovered in 1931, it drew people and profit to the town like never before. Only for a while. The population dropped again by the time I was an older teenager and became small enough so that we always felt as if we knew everyone.

Uncle Geiger raised strawberries when I was a child, and the red berries spread over hill and dale as far as I could see. One day he let us crawl under his fence to pick some strawberries and I never tasted anything as good. He was a straight-laced character and fit into the more reserved Haire side of my family as the husband of my Aunt Ella. He drove a Model-T car that could hit 45mph with a good tailwind, and we loved it when he let us take rides in it once in a while. That car was so light and cute that it only took a few of us to pick it up with our bare hands, and that came in handy if the car ever got stuck in the mud!

I never volunteered for inside chores (other than washing dishes so I could listen to an episode of *Stella Dallas*). I much preferred working outside with my dad. My family members were my playmates. We made up games and often played house in a little clearing we built in the woods near our home. I swept it clean every day and we pretended to cook meals just like Mother, only our kitchen stove was on the rocks in our playhouse. My Aunt Gazelle from Tyler and her two children seemed to have more—or at least spend more—than my family did. My aunt dressed her kids Allen and Ann in white shorts, shirts, and shoes like a fairytale princess and little Lord Fauntleroy. On the other hand, I ran around barefoot as often as I could. I played hard every day in whatever clothes I happened to throw on in the morning and stayed in them until dark. I'll never forget one day when my cousins came to visit us. I was in the playhouse cooking two eggs that I had found. I had built a fire and was heating the eggs on some bricks, pretending I was in my fancy kitchen making a gourmet meal for my guests. The eggs were pretty, but they were also rotten. We were all playing along having a grand time when the rotten eggs suddenly exploded. The mess got all over my cousin Ann's perfectly starched outfit and dripped off her hair and face. She stunk to high heaven and screamed bloody murder back to the house to tell our mothers! I got in trouble, but it was worth it.

Daddy was a strong man with an even stronger personality. One time my uncle crossed the line and found out just how strong my father was. Daddy was off at work when Uncle Virgil got in a fight with Al who was a teen by then. I don't know what they were arguing about, but Uncle Virgil slapped Al so hard across the face that it left a mark. Of course, we couldn't wait to tell Daddy what Uncle Virgil had done to Al and counted the hours until we heard Daddy's pickup pull into the driveway. Uncle Virgil happened to be walking toward our house about the time we told Daddy about the fight, probably to give his side of the story. But it was too late. Daddy flew into Uncle Virgil and beat the tar out of him right in front of all of us in the middle of the road! Then Daddy just calmly turned on his heel and walked home. We all learned a lesson that day. Nobody messed with Daddy's children.

But Daddy had a softer side, too. The same dark, rough hands that whipped our bottoms when we were wrong were gentle enough to cut all our hair on the front porch. But the thing is he used farm tools and they hurt!

America was struggling through the Great Depression when I was a child. Hobos often camped out in a little hovel along the railroad that ran along the highway directly in front of our home. What I saw around that railroad looked like scenes straight out of *The Grapes of Wrath*. Families with nothing but the clothes on their backs and men pushing wheelbarrows with their belongings lined the tracks. They never did cross the highway to set up their ramshackle homes and tents near us but stayed close to the railroad ties. Whenever those men and their families came to our door asking for food, Daddy never turned away anyone. He often gave them small jobs to do around the house, picking fruit or helping him with the fields.

One of the poorest ladies I met who lived by the railroad was named Miss Rose—a long, thin woman who was so nice to us. She always wanted to do something for my mother to repay our family's kindness and even offered to milk our cow one day. This was fine by me because our Jersey cow was mean. I watched as Miss Rose walked into our pasture, and the next thing I saw was our bull charging right at her! I saw her skinny arms and legs flailing as quickly as they could go to get away from him. She was picking them up high and putting them down fast. Needless to say, that chore landed squarely back in my lap that day.

It was my job to milk our cow before I went to school each day and in the evening before I went to bed. I didn't mind doing it, except the cow truly was meaner than a snake. She kicked every time I tried to milk her, and one day she even knocked over the fresh bucket of milk I'd just filled up. I was so mad at her for doing that. Snatching up my empty pail to show Daddy, I stomped over to the house and told him what the cow had done. He did not say a word but set down his coffee cup and left through the back door heading to the barn. Daddy and this cow had an understanding after he got her by the tail and somehow flipped her over on her back. "There, milk her now," Daddy announced. He went back to the kitchen, leaving me standing there holding my empty milk bucket with my mouth wide open.

My siblings and I also collected eggs every day and swept the yard with brooms made from broken branches we found among the pines in the woods. Why we had to sweep the dirt in front of our house I will never know. But Mother liked it that way and we couldn't stand to disappoint her.

Arp had a handful of churches, stores, and streets in

the small downtown area. There was a bank, a post office, and our school was down from our house. Near our home was also a honky tonk that I now know was also a brothel. But I had no idea what that was back then. My parents let us trade eggs with the painted ladies at the back door, but Daddy firmly instructed us not to *ever* go inside there. And we didn't. We handed our eggs to the madam who answered the door, collected money from her, and hightailed it back home as if the devil himself were chasing us. But I desperately wanted to know what they did in there.

One day I delivered eggs and mustered up enough courage to ask the madam to tell me what went on behind that door. She smiled and agreed to tell me. My eyes grew wide as I listened, and I turned around and left before she finished talking. I ran twice as fast as usual all the way back through the field to our house. Suddenly a familiar voice caught me by surprise. I stopped and jumped straight up in the air as if I'd been stung by a bee.

"Did you talk to those women?"

I whipped around to see Mother standing there, hands on her hips with eyes blazing. How she knew what I'd done I'll never know. There was nothing for me to do but to tell the truth.

"Yes ma'am. I sure did," I confessed. And I never opened my mouth at the brothel again.

I also took fresh milk to the red-bricked Harmon house on the hill each week, a wealthy family who owned everything we lived on. They had a pond we called the Harmon pond because it was all theirs—imagine! A whole pond of your own! It had the most beautiful white sand and the cleanest water bubbling up from a spring that was the best stuff you ever put to your lips.

I earned a dollar a week milking our cow and carefully saved my money so that I could buy something nice like a pair of Buster Brown shoes. Like Stella Dallas, I daydreamed of someday being able to put my mother in the Harmon's beautiful hilltop mansion. Their house was many times larger than ours and their grounds had some of the most beautiful trees dotting their property. Sometimes when I walked through the pasture hauling my bucket of milk to their back door I would get lost in my thoughts. I would think to myself, "What if this was my mother's house? What if this was our backdoor? What if those were our trees? Wouldn't Mother be proud!" I never knew anyone who had the kind of money the Harmons had. They were very good to our family. And even though we lived on the same side of the railroad, we came from different sides of the track.

I remember Mother made me a new dress when I was a teenager, and I thought it was the prettiest I'd ever seen. When the Harmons invited me over to attend a party one day, I knew I wanted to wear it. Brushing my hair until it was glossy, I put on my new dress and the best shoes I had. At the time, I never wore make up like the rest of the girls my age did. I didn't want that stuff on my face and never would have slowed down long enough to put it on anyway—not even for the Harmon party. Checking my appearance one last time in the mirror, I started my walk through the pasture to their home. When I got to their property, like the tomboy I was, I roughly hiked up my hem to crawl over the fence in their front yard. When I straightened up, their daughter Charlotte suddenly turned the water hose on me and completely ruined my hair and my dress. My face turned red and I saw everyone staring at me. I could tell they felt sorry for me, and I hated that feeling. It broke my heart. I was so embarrassed that I turned and crawled back through the fence and ran home crying. That night as I lay in bed, I wondered why I'd ever dreamed of being like the Harmons.

On Saturdays Mrs. Harmon would sometimes call

our home to invite us to the movies. "The chauffer will pick you up and take you to the movie if you want to go," she'd say. My siblings and I couldn't tumble out of our three-room house fast enough to pile into the jump seats of their Cadillac for the quick trip to one of Overton's several movie theaters. We thought we had arrived! It seems like small towns like Overton and Arp had more movie theaters than people during those days when the oil money was flowing freely.

The Harmons were different from us in every way. We were country people and they were high class. Their children didn't go to school in Arp or nearby New London like most of my friends did. Although we had good schools because of the oil money in our area, the Harmon kids went off to school somewhere else to places I had never heard of and they lived lives that we could only imagine.

We felt more at home with a man we called Uncle Thomas who also lived on the Harmon property. He had been a slave of Mrs. Wilson, the mother of Mrs. Harmon. She had brought him with her when her family moved to Arp. Uncle Thomas worked doing odd jobs on the Harmon property, but he was set up like a king with a nice home and a good salary. He could do just about anything that needed doing on their farm. We didn't know how old he was, but we loved Uncle Thomas as if he were our own family. I remember looking at his yellow thumbnails that were so thick from plucking chickens all his life. Whenever we visited Uncle Thomas, he would invite us in and open a big wooden trunk. It must have carried all his belongings at one time but was now filled with a variety of candy he kept on hand just for us. "Get you some candy," he'd say with a smile and we would fill our pockets until they were stuffed.

It almost killed all of us the day Uncle Thomas died. Our whole family attended the funeral with the Harmons and I cried myself to sleep that night. Over the years I've gone to see Uncle Thomas' grave in Sinclair City, Texas, remembering his kindness to all of us.

Although I thought about the Harmon family a lot when I was young, I loved the way that I grew up and wouldn't trade it for anything. But I do remember all the times I quietly wished for something my family could not afford. And I sometimes wondered what it would be like to buy my parents anything they wanted.

My father's family did not have money, but my mother's parents lived near us in Arp in a large home on some property. When I was older, I would discover that one of the reasons Daddy drank was to try to ease the pain he felt over something that had happened with my grandparents long ago when Daddy and Mother married. I did not know the full story until much later, but when I learned the truth, I understood my father much better.

MONEY WAS TIGHT IN our family, but my parents made sure there was more than enough love to make up for it. My Daddy worked so hard for everything we had. He often worked at the sugar cane mill on the side to earn extra money. A pair of mules would walk in circles moving a heavy grinder to mash the cane stalks in order to make the sweet syrup.

Options were few in my small town, and I knew I would also have to work hard for what I wanted from life like he did. At the same time, I knew that I wouldn't mind working hard to get ahead. But for some reason I began telling myself whenever I walked to school or did my chores, "This is just today. Tomorrow I'm going to

be something else." I don't know what made me think
that way. But the feeling was so strong. Looking back
on those days, I truly believed from the beginning that
somehow God had something in mind for me. I knew
my life would turn out different someday, but I did not
know exactly how to get there.

Charlotte and the Harmon family finally moved
south to San Antonio when I was older. In time, their
beautiful house that once seemed like a plantation home
in *Gone with the Wind*, slowly began aging. It was even
abandoned for many years after Mrs. Wilson died there.

Much later when I was married with a family of my
own, I had the unexpected opportunity of having some
money. One of the first things I wanted to do was to
buy the Harmon property—all one hundred acres,
including the old Harmon homestead. Mother was a
widow by then and my father had been dead a long time.
I initially thought that my mother would want to move
in the house just like I'd planned for so many years. But
we looked at it together one day and saw that it had lost
a lot of its charm. First of all, it was not nearly as large or
as nice as I'd remembered it being. The grand stairwell
with all the elegant Harmon portraits was long gone.
And the home had long since been cut up, remodeled,

and repaired in odd ways over many years.

It's funny. When I had the chance to make something I'd dreamed about most of my life come true, suddenly I didn't want it at all. Life can change you that way. If Mother had wanted the house, of course, I would have worked it out to make that happen. Thankfully, she didn't want to live there either after we saw the state it was in. We walked out of the front door, and I saw our old house down the hill to the right. That was home. Our home. This place had only been a dream. We went back to our car and never thought about the Harmon house again.

We looked at another home for her in Arp across the street from the cemetery, but it mysteriously burned to the ground two weeks later in an electrical fire. We had been right at the point of buying it when this happened, and Mother said later that God was looking out for us. We soon ran out of options for her in Arp, so I eventually bought my mother a home just minutes from me in Tyler. It was in a neighborhood overlooking a small private lake. I had such fun decorating it myself, including ordering all the furniture and placing all the accessories in just the right spots. When she walked in her new home for the first time, I took a breath and proudly announced, "It's all yours. And you don't have to pay a penny." Mother was quiet. She walked over to the window and sat in a comfortable chair I'd picked out for her. For the next few minutes she just looked around and asked me over and over, "Is this really my house?"

Yes, I told her, it was all hers. God gave her several more years with us after that, and I treasured every moment we had together. I only wished it could have been longer.

CHAPTER TWO

# Life in Arp

Whee I was growing up, we swam in anything that had water in it. I practically learned to swim before I could walk. We loved going to my grandfather's house to swim in a community swimming pool he'd built on their property. I can't begin to tell you how big this spring-fed pool was—it was something out of this world for me to get to go there. It was the first of its kind in East Texas and had beach sand all around it, a high dive, a zip-line into the water, and a beautiful bathhouse with swimsuits for everyone. My grandfather charged a small admission fee for the upkeep, and it was a real treat for everyone in the surrounding towns to play at the pool and escape the summer heat. Sometimes my brothers skinny-dipped after hours when it was closed to the public. My favorite trick was to sneak up on the boys while they were busy playing and hide their clothes! Somehow they always knew it was me. All of us have fond family memories at that pool. Daddy loved jumping off the high-dive and we spent many an hour trying to dunk Daddy and each other under the water.

Daddy had two mules to help him work, and he let us ride on a gentle mare we called Nelly Bell. She was a beautiful plow horse with a rusty red coat and white splotches. We rode her five or six kids at a time when we were young and she never minded. She was like another sibling to us—always in the middle of all our fun. One time several of us rode her over to a dam on the Harmon property after a hard rain. The dam had broken and pools of water created several pot holes in the mud that we could not see. Suddenly Nelly Bell stepped into one of the low spots, and it sucked her legs into the thick mud right up to her belly. We screamed and my siblings and

I slid off her back. We tried pulling her out every which way we could pull, but Nelly Bell wouldn't budge. We pulled her by the neck (and even her tail) to encourage her to step out of it. But she just sank lower into the muck. I finally had the idea of building a small fire near her to scare her out and would you believe it worked! We were careful not to burn her tail, but Daddy burned our tails when we got home because we were absolutely caked in mud, Nelly Bell too.

Daddy whipped us with a leather shaving strap whenever we deserved it. There was always plenty of blame to go around with ten children, all with a mind of their own. If nobody confessed, Daddy would line us up and whip each one just for good measure.

Play time after school was my favorite. I loved to go home on occasion with one of my friends named Imogene Hartley because she had a refrigerator and we got to eat Post Toasties cereal with cold milk. When I was about eleven years, I often walked downtown after school to Mr. Robert Wilson's general store. He had a wheel of cheddar cheese out on the counter under a glass cover and it seemed to call my name every time I went in there. There was nothing that tasted as good as a wedge of that delicious cheddar cheese. One day I decided to buy me a slice and charge it to Daddy's account. Mr. Wilson raised his eyebrows, but he wrote down the charge in a little notebook he kept and let me have the cheese. I ate it as I walked home, and it tasted so good that I went back the next day and did it again. I did that I don't know how many times.

When Daddy came in Mr. Wilson's store to pay the grocery bill at the end of the month, he was in for a surprise. And so was I. Daddy came home that afternoon and threw the bill down on the table. "Somebody's been liking some cheese," he said, pointing his gaze straight at me. I was so nervous and I smiled weakly. He didn't smile. "I'm going out to the barn and I will be back to tend to you in a little bit." He should have beat me right then because waiting for it to happen was agony.

Since Daddy was gone a lot of the time, Mother had her own way of dealing with us when we got in trouble. We had to pick the switch off the tree that she would use to punish us. I always took an extra minute to choose one that seemed like it wouldn't hurt as much. But pulling our hair was worse than being spanked with a switch. That was Mother's secret weapon to get our attention in a hurry.

The worst whipping I ever received had to be the time

I took a nickel that had fallen out of a teacher's bag. I pocketed it and bought a hamburger for lunch from the who lady cooked hamburgers every day next to our schoolhouse. For the last few minutes of class, the smell of those grilled burgers came through the open windows and nearly tortured us. When the school bell rang for lunch, you could run as fast as you could to the hamburger stand, but you couldn't be quick enough to be first in line. We usually walked the half-mile home from school for lunch because our family didn't have money to waste. But that day I saw the shiny nickel on the ground and treated myself to a burger. I felt so guilty later about stealing it and thought about what I'd done for days. As it turns out, my cousin Ruth was the teacher who lost the nickel. Worse yet, someone saw me take it and told on me. My father made sure I learned a lesson from this experience. You should never take anything that doesn't belong to you.

The first teachers I remember having were Miss Ruth and Miss Mink. We met for school in a two-story wood building with four grades per room. I don't remember much, but I do know that I had a crush back then on Charles Rhodes who lived by the overpass, and penmanship was my favorite subject. We practiced our letters using a dark slate and white chalk. It was a big deal when we received new Big Red paper tablets in second grade, and we wrote in them using cedar pencils that my dad would sharpen with his pocket knife.

MOTHER WAS OFTEN SICK when I was younger. We did everything we could to make her better, and finally Daddy brought her to the new Mother Frances Hospital in Tyler. This state-of-the-art hospital opened early when the New London school exploded from a natural gas leak in 1937 just minutes before school let out. No one knew that the highly volatile and odorless gas had been collecting in such great volume that it literally blew the roof off the school and leveled the building. I'll never forget that day. The girl who lived across the street from us had a brother who went to school in New London, along with several hundred other students. I was playing in the front yard when she told me what happened and then she asked if I wanted to go see it. I was only twelve years old and the memories of what I saw have haunted me ever since.

I don't know why I didn't have a nervous breakdown afterwards. It was horrible. I saw so many victims—children like me—laying out on the ground dead. Their twisted faces were gray, and their hair was matted from the ash that rained down in the explosion. Almost 300 people were killed instantly and at least as many were injured. My friend and her family members were shouting their brother's name, growing more frantic by the minute. They finally found his body, but they could only identify him by a ring he was wearing.

People felt the explosion as far as 40 miles away. Everyone stopped whatever they were doing throughout the area and came over to help look for survivors and recover the dead. Parents, farmers, roughnecks, and men in ties and dress shirts worked tirelessly side by side using their bare hands and peach baskets to carry away debris and body parts in a desperate search that went on for several days.

Daddy, along with many other oil field workers, was one of those who volunteered to help. He worked for three days and nights straight recovering bodies. He never stopped, even to change clothes. I remember Mother telling us how Daddy had found the head of one of the teachers who was also the aunt of a young man we knew. Everyone knew someone who was killed that day in New London. Dozens of delivery trucks and pickups took the bodies away to funeral homes all over East Texas because there were not enough ambulances. We went to sixteen funerals in one day. They would put one coffin on the altar and have a service, then they'd take that one out and put another coffin in in its place. It was like that for hours.

Letters of condolence and telegrams arrived from all over the nation and dozens of countries, including one from the early days of Adolf Hitler before he showed what a madman he was. Thankfully, leaders the world over agreed to add a foul-smelling agent to natural gas to avoid another tragedy like the New London explosion.

Arp and East Texas became famous overnight for another event in history when notorious bank robbers Bonnie and Clyde robbed the refinery in Arp and drove away with all the cash stuffed into their 1933 Ford. Uncle Jack, who was married to Aunt Gazelle, worked at the refinery. They held him at gunpoint, kidnapped and stripped him of his clothes, and left him out in the country to walk back to town. He was lucky to be alive! When Bonnie and Clyde were killed in a hail of gunfire in 1934, I was eleven years old. As a show of victory, local law enforcement paraded the robbers' shot-up Ford through our town and across East Texas. We paid a nickel to see it when it came through Arp!

Two doctors had lived on either side of our home before we moved there. One was named Dr. Creel and my baby brother was named Billy Creel after him. When Daddy bought our house from the Harmons, it was on the other side of the highway. He asked if he could move the small pier-and-beam home across the street under a great oak tree that was growing in what would become our front yard. Daddy had scouted out that location for our home so the tree could provide us with cool shade in the hot Texas summers.

Ours was a shotgun style house, meaning you could see all the way through to the back when you walked in the front. It had a long porch on the side where we slept outside on cool evenings and took baths in a metal washtub in warm summers. In the winter, Mother moved the washtub near the wood-burning stove so that nobody would catch pneumonia, and I helped Daddy cut wood to stack beside the stove. We drew water from a well for everything we needed, from bathwater to cooking water.

Behind our house was a short path with a bathroom at the end of it. We called it an outhouse. Mother stocked our outhouse with pages of the *Sears & Roebuck* catalog to use as toilet paper. One time I talked one of my sisters into helping me get some eggs out of our chickens' nests and dropped them in the toilet. We hid and watched from behind a tree when Al went in there. He came out running, so excited to tell Mother that he'd found the missing eggs she'd been looking for. I was mad because he got all the glory, and it was all my doing!

We knew to seek shelter in our outdoor storm cellar whenever a strong thunderstorm headed our way. East Texas is notorious for spring storms when the sky turns a scary shade of blackish grey, and even the birds hide. I remember my brothers and sisters running out of the house toward the cellar one afternoon during such a storm. I was still on the porch when a powerful gust of wind nearly picked me up and carried me to the cellar. One spring a storm blew away the red barn on our property where Daddy loved to work.

Daddy taught all my brothers how to use a gun and how to make traps for hunting. He was also good at making home brew. When he was younger, he made moonshine behind our house in a little building we called the smoke shack. Daddy smoked meats in there but at some point he stopped doing that and started brewing beer. If you shook one of Daddy's homemade bottles of beer too hard it would explode in your hand. I sometimes heard the lids of his collection of glass bottles popping off at night like firecrackers. He also kept whiskey buried in various places by the smoke shack so that Mother wouldn't find it. My grown children have found several flasks on our Arp property over the years since Daddy's death. He kept these bottles out of Mother's sight so she wouldn't see him drinking, but I have an idea that she always knew more than she let on.

My parents and many of my family members are buried in the Mason cemetery in Arp. My children like to bring up the time when we visited my grandparents' grave and I nearly fell into the fresh grave of George Driver—the local crazy man everyone knew in Arp. He may have been strange and he certainly walked slowly, but I didn't mind. I liked him and, besides, he was always nice to me. As I child I even got the chance to practice my nursing skills on George when he came by our house one day. He and Dad were visiting when George suddenly took his shoes and socks off and showed Daddy how swollen his big toe was. I was pretending not to notice, but that toe of his was fascinating. "Louise, go get the coal oil and doctor his toe," my dad instructed me. I tore my eyes away from George's toe and jumped up to get the dark bottle of liquid we used as a cure-all for any ailment. I doctored George's toe and imagined I was a nurse treating my patient.

The only other medicine our family ever used besides coal oil was castor oil and something we called "three sixes" for colds. Mother made us take big doses of three sixes at least once a year. It was an herb that honestly looked like marijuana to me, but Mother mixed it with syrup and we forced it down our throats. She would let us chase the bitter taste with orange slices if we had some on hand, but most of the time we just had to drink it straight. It could cure anything, but it almost made me sicker to swallow it. Daddy preferred hot toddies when he had a cough, and I still remember the strong, spicy smell of warm whiskey and peppermint sticks slowly melting in it.

❧

MY ROLE IN OUR family was to make everyone laugh. I always felt that I was responsible for making everything okay and taking care of everyone. Maybe it sprang from all the times I took care of Daddy on the front porch. There were times when it became stressful at home because Mother was so sick and Daddy was breaking his back to provide for us. I tried to lighten Mother's mood by making her laugh whenever I was sure that she felt more like crying. Mother went through periods when she was bed-ridden and couldn't take care of our home or even cook meals. Jean and I stepped in during those times and became "mom" to our younger siblings who looked to us to take care of their needs.

For a while, I believed Mother thought Jean was an angel and that I was the devil. I really did. I was such a prankster and got away with murder many times. Jean, on the other hand, was industrious and stayed up late doing productive things like darning her socks. I can just see her now, stretching them one at a time over a light bulb while she sewed the holes. My socks always had holes in them, so I would sneak Jean's out of her dresser drawer and wear them to school instead of my own.

As the oldest, Jean was a very straight-laced woman her whole life. We were proud when she graduated from nursing school in San Antonio 300 miles away from Arp. I took a bus to see her at school a couple of times, but Jean promptly sent me back home each time! She thought all I ever wanted to do was have fun, and she didn't need me distracting her from her studies.

The truth is that I would have given anything to become a nurse like Jean, but I was not smart in school. I had common sense and enjoyed history, but I was not necessarily book smart. I made Bs and Cs and was glad to get them. I wasn't interested in school then. I was too busy.

Jean was smart. But one thing we discovered early on when Mother was sick was that I was better at cooking. Of course, no one was better than my mom, but when we needed a meal on the table, I could make something as well as anyone. Like Mother, I did not follow a recipe but always put it together in my head, trying a little of this and a little of that. I've cooked that way all my life and rarely measured any ingredients.

As a teen, I'd go outside to our garden and pick peas, tomatoes, and onions and make us a feast. I learned to cook cornbread from scratch and often even had a simple cake or pie for dessert. Many times our whole family worked in the field to help Daddy work his crops, and I'd leave in time to go back home and fix us lunch, which we called dinner. I packed everything up and brought the food outside to them. We sat out underneath a big tree and ate together in the shade enjoying sweet potatoes, fried chicken, corn bread, or pole bread. Sometimes Mother's brother Johnny would join us and that was always a treat.

My specialty became chicken and dumplings. I had watched Mother wring a chicken's neck in the yard when I was little, but thank goodness when I was older we could just go to the store and buy chicken. I tried wringing a chicken's neck one time—and one time only. I grabbed the poor bird, swung it around a few times like Mother had shown me, and laid it down. But the bird jumped up and ran off with his neck cocked sideways and feathers spilling everywhere!

When we were old enough to work, all the children got paying jobs to help support the family. Everyone was expected to work back then and do their part. My first job was in my teens working for a drive-in café in Overton. I had lots of experience in the kitchen by then and knew how to cook for a large group of hungry people in a hurry. I knew early on that I could never be stuck away in an office job—I enjoy meeting and talking with people too much. I had a ball cooking hamburgers on the grill and making sandwiches in that little café. I later worked at Neil-Simpson's Drugstore on Broadway in downtown Tyler at the soda fountain and have fond memories of making milkshakes for all of my friends.

Al—the firstborn son, my playmate, and Daddy's assistant—worked hard plowing the ground alongside Daddy, while I busied myself throwing red dirt clods at him from my favorite hiding spots. One time I accidentally hit Daddy square in the face with a dirt clod and that was the end of that game. Al could do anything—pulling the ground sled behind Nelly Bell to smooth the dirt and then working in the barn on projects until sunset.

When the United States entered World War II, Al was only sixteen years old. But he stretched the truth so that he could join the Navy and serve our country. We all went down to the train station to tell him goodbye when he went off to war. As the engine pulled away, I broke away from my family and ran alongside the train car calling out to Al, "Be sure to put your insurance in my name!" Everyone laughed, including Al. But our laughter was only temporary. No one knew how far away from home the Navy would take our Al. And we had no idea if we'd ever see him alive again.

Al was gone for almost two years serving in the South Pacific on the USS Fergus. He fought in the Philippines and Guam, including the bloody Battle of Okinawa. Al later said on many occasions that he "grew up" in the South Pacific. By the time he came home, anyone could see that the sixteen-year-old boy had now become a young man.

Mother treasured every letter Al wrote home. But he did not write her nearly enough. One time when he went a good while without writing, Mother asked me to sit down and help her draft a letter to his commanding officer. In the letter, she politely asked that the officer please tell her son to write his mother! She would presume Al was dead, she told me to say, if she did not hear from him soon.

It wasn't long before Mother got a long letter of apology from Al, written while his commanding officer stood over his shoulder. After spending three days in the brig on bread and water, Al never again let too many weeks go by without writing home.

⁘

BECAUSE JEAN, AL, AND I were the oldest, our parents often let us walk into town together in the early evening. I have many memories of walking home past Lingo Leaper lumber company and other businesses. These old buildings became as familiar to me as the trees along the way. We always stopped at the lumber company to drink ice-cold water they kept in a wooden barrel with a spout. After church we'd walk along the railroad track across from our home and follow it all the way to the cemetery. That property was dotted with white gardenia flowers during the spring and their strong smell always permeated the air. A time was coming, and soon, when I would return to that cemetery, but it would not be by choice.

Whenever we walked near the railroad, we would look for stumps of almost-burnt up flares that the railroad engineers tossed out the window of the train.

My siblings and I could not wait to make a small fire with them. Finding one was like Christmas morning. Al, Jean, and I would walk beside fields of ribbon cane growing on either side of the highway and make up games to pass the time. When we grew bored one day watching a man named Mr. Stamps plow the field for Daddy we got into some mischief. Mr. Stamps was Daddy's right hand man and he often paid him to help him with his farming. Jean and Al and I dug up an old rotted piece of wood and for some reason decided to throw it at Mr. Stamps. It hit him in the rear end, and we realized right away that we could have hurt him, so we ran. He told my father what happened of course, and we all learned a good lesson that night from Daddy.

I felt safe with Al and Jean nearby whenever we walked home in the evenings, even though I hated walking through the dark woods and up the drive to our house at night. The branches were so thick with leaves that they blocked the moon, and I was afraid someone or something would grab me. I never went in those woods by myself at night.

Sometimes Charlie would go with us on these adventures into town or to the cemetery. Charlie looked as handsome as John Kennedy to me. He was a wonderful young man, but he developed brain cancer when we were both older with families of our own. I walked over to his house near mine in Tyler every day when he got sick. When I lost Charlie, I thought my heart would break because I loved him so.

Ellen was my beautiful redhead younger sister, a trait she inherited from my mother's side of the family—as did Al and Jean. Mother was not a true redhead, but her hair glistened a little in the sun if you looked at her just right. Ellen, like our older sister, was also very smart and graduated from Tyler Junior College with honors. Mother's parents made Ellen take piano lessons when she was young. Ellen had a natural ear for music and could sit at the piano and play anything she wanted. We always had a piano in our home, and I remember the times Mother and my sister sang and played together. Ellen eventually married a man from Fort Worth who was in the Service when she was pregnant, and I'll never forget being there with her when her little boy was born.

Ann was the youngest girl in our family and a true Southern lady. She was the baby girl and was often sick when she was little. I stayed with her in the hospital many times, trying to distract her from her pain and keep her entertained. Daddy was so proud when Billy

Creel, the baby boy and last child, was born. He said, "I've got me a big boy with black hair, cowboy boots and everything." Billy was special to all of us.

My best friend in high school was named Thelma. Thelma and Louise, we were always together. She would do absolutely anything that anyone dared her to do, even though her parents were Pentecostal and very conservative. I thought it was strange when Thelma told me that she couldn't wear shorts. I made sure to remember to bring her some of mine to wear at school for volleyball or P.E. class. And she made sure her parents didn't find out.

One time Thelma and I decided that we wanted to go to an out-of-town football game. The only problem was that we didn't have a ride. We'd already been told there was no room on the bus with the school band, so we decided to hitchhike the few miles to the next town. Would you believe the first pickup to come over the hill and see us standing there beside the road belonged to Daddy? We never made it to the football game that night, needless to say.

In high school some of the bad crowd got into drinking alcohol. It was not easy to get their hands on it unlike today. But I remember several boys coming to class some mornings bragging about their hangovers. I smoked later when I was a young adult—everyone did in those days, even all the movie stars—but I never have liked the taste of alcohol very much. It scared me to see what it did to Daddy.

Thelma and I eventually grew apart when we were older—life sometimes takes you down different paths. But I will never forget our adventures together in a time when it was so easy to have such fun with so little.

DADDY WAS A HARD worker all his life. He fought the unions who began taking over all the jobs until it was pitiful. When he finally retired, it seemed like that event marked the moment when he started to change. He finally found the Lord ten or twelve years before he died. I knew something was different the day that my husband and I went to Arp to visit my parents and found Daddy sitting in his chair with his Bible open. I had never seen my father with a Bible and did not know he even had one. I tried to hide my surprise because I didn't want to embarrass him. Mother looked over and gave me a quick smile without saying a word. She knew I was amazed. When we left, I cried all the way back to Tyler because I realized that God had changed Daddy from the inside out when we weren't even looking. God sometimes does His best work like that—behind the scenes and just when you think He is not doing anything.

When my father became sick near the end of his life, I drove to Arp to pick him up and take him to his doctor appointments in Tyler. He talked with me on these visits in a way I'd always wanted him to talk to me all of my life. I think he sensed that he had reached the end of the road and that our time together was growing short. We laughed and told family stories, just the two of us, all the way there and back many times.

"Is there anything between you and the Lord that you need to take care of?" I asked him one day.

This was about three weeks before his death, but I did not know that then. My dad had lived hard and rough most of his life, although he loved each of us with a tender heart. He'd privately carried so much heartache and had tried his best to shield us from it. I often thought of the nights on our front porch when he was too drunk to go inside for fear of the rest of the family seeing him that way. But now when I looked at the gentle old man sitting beside me in the car, all that pain seemed to be a lifetime ago.

He just smiled at me and said, "Not a thing, Louise. Not a thing."

When he died, I was at peace with his relationship with God, and I believe he was too. My mother never gave up praying that my dad would one day find God. And he did. I don't know how many tears she must have cried over him or how many prayers she prayed. But I learned one thing for certain from Mother—we should never give up on something that we really desire with all our heart. Truth be told, we seldom really expect much in prayer. But we always get a lot. Even if it's not always what we asked for. Occasionally I lie down on my bed and wake up later with a troublesome pain. I ask God to take it away and sometimes He does. But sometimes He doesn't. I don't really know why He does one thing and not another. God always answers prayer, but we all must realize that He usually takes His time.

BECAUSE OF MOTHER, I went to church every day of my life when I was younger. There were churches on every corner in the tiny community of Arp. Although Daddy stayed home, Mother made sure we went as a family to every church in town. There wasn't anything else to do with our time, and there was always a revival going on at the Methodist or Baptist church. The Pentecostal church was also a good one to go to because there was a woman there who would invariably "get holy" at some point in the service and dance all over the place. My siblings and I would try not to laugh because we knew Mother was at the ready, sitting just arm's length away on the same pew with us. She could and would pinch us by the hair on the nape of our necks if we so much as giggled. I took a girlfriend with me to that church one night to show her the dancing woman and to make fun. To my surprise my friend ended up finding the Lord that night! I've been told that Mother once took us to hear a young man preaching a crusade in Tyler. She enjoyed it so much and I wish like anything that I had been older so I could say that I remember the day Billy Graham preached in East Texas.

I'd watched many baptism services from the safety of the banks of a little pond from the time that I was small. I always begged my mother to let me get baptized too. I was just a child and too little for that act to mean something to me at the time. But I was awfully anxious to do what I'd seen everyone else doing. When I was older I finally convinced her that I was ready, and I got to get in the pond one Sunday afternoon after church. I stepped into the warm water and felt my toes sink into the cold mud on the bottom as I reached for the hand of the preacher who would baptize me. Everyone clapped and Mother was so happy for me afterwards. Yet when I came out of the water, I was disappointed that I felt no different than when I'd gone in. It didn't mean one thing to me. Nevertheless, God was working on me even then.

All of her life, my mother prayed earnestly for each of her children to know God, and she was truly the finest Christian woman I've ever known. All of Mother's aunts were also good Christian examples for me. I saw Aunt Jean, Aunt Ella, and Aunt Gazelle reading their Bibles and praying many times throughout my childhood.

This made an impression on me that I could not forget. Daddy's family was also Christian, even though one of his sisters could also cuss a blue streak!

The Bible talks about generations of families serving Him, and this was certainly true in my family. My grandparents taught my mother to be a Christian, my mother taught us, and then I taught my children to know the Lord, too.

When you are a teenager, you often feel things and think about life on a deeper level than you do when you become an adult. I had a deep love for the Lord, even before I knew what that was all about and long before I ever became a Christian. When I was in my first year in high school, those feelings deepened. I felt drawn to God in ways that I could not explain. Between Mother and the Pentecostal church, I'd heard so much about God by then that I decided I wanted to be a Christian for real this time. I wasn't too sure about all the jumping and dancing around that the Pentecostals did. But, I told myself, maybe God wouldn't make me do all that if I didn't want to. One Sunday I walked down the center aisle at church after the service to tell the pastor that I wanted to be a Christian. Walking home that day I felt so good about my decision to trust Christ as my Savior.

I became even closer to God after that, and I remember many times wanting to run to the woods during the day just so I could get alone and pray. There was always something happening in our home with so many family members going in and out of it, so you had to get away in order to be by yourself for more than a minute. I'd walk to a field on a path near our home where there were always butterflies flitting about and bees building hives in the trees. It's funny how your mind can grab a memory that long ago and you find it's all still there as if it were yesterday. This became my favorite spot where I could kneel in the cool grass and pray, feeling the warm sunshine on my face. Somehow, I knew God was real in those moments. I would never do everything right in my life, but I always knew He was near me.

⸙

MOTHER'S STRONG FAITH MEANS even more to me now because I realize how much she must have suffered when she was sick during my childhood. I never knew exactly what was wrong with her. None of the doctors seemed to know what to do either, including the specialists we took her to in Tyler.

We were used to these strange weak spells, but one particular night was different. The Arp doctor was at her bedside that evening and quietly informed my father that Mother was close to death. My siblings were crying and none of us could believe this news. I was terrified that I would lose my mother any minute. I went out on our porch under the moonlight and dug my nails into the wood on the front railing, fighting back tears. Why would God take my mother? I could not imagine what would happen to our family without her. She was the center of our world. Who would take us in? What would Daddy do? I did not even want to think about what it would do to my father to lose my mother.

Suddenly I remembered that it was Sunday night and the Pentecostals were having a church service. Without telling anyone where I was going, I ran across our yard and made my way in the pitch dark through the woods to the church. I saw a dim light in the distance and ran as fast as I could toward it, trying not to let my fear of being alone in those woods at night slow me down. I burst through the front door and interrupted their service to ask them to please come pray for my mother. I must have been quite the sight. My face was red and sweaty and my hair was a wild mess. I'd somehow brushed against barbed wire in my race to the church, and a red stream of blood was running down my leg from a jagged gash on my knee. The whole church turned out that night at my house to pray for my mother. They gathered around in a big circle outside our home and prayed with loud cries for God to heal her. We watched from a distance and waited.

I washed the deep wound on my knee as best as I could in the kitchen, watching the red blood wash down the drain and listening to the townspeople praying outside the window deep into the night. I should have gotten stitches, but that was the last thing on anyone's mind. The next morning my mom got up from her bed for the first time in weeks. I still have a long scar on my knee from that night to remind me of the wonderful power of prayer.

## CHAPTER THREE

# Forbidden Love

My family called my grandmother Emma Herrington on my daddy's side "Black Dutch." But she wasn't Dutch or black—it was just how people described darker-skinned Europeans in their family tree. I did a home DNA test kit one time and was surprised to learn that I am British. But I like to think of myself as the girl from Arp. That's who I am, and it's the way I want to be remembered.

Daddy's mom was barely five feet tall, if that, and we

all called her Little Emma to distinguish her from my
other grandmother who was also named Emma. Despite
her small stature, we all respected that feisty fistful of
fire. If you crossed Little Emma she would thunder all
over you before you could blink. I remember one time I
was playing with Pappy under a tree and having the best
time when she came out there and grabbed him by the
shirt collar. She turned it inside out and said, "Lem, you
need a bath!" I was dancing around him doing my best to
distract him from the bad news that she'd pronounced
when she suddenly slapped me silly. I was so shocked
that I did not cry. I was mad and wanted to hit her back,
but I knew better than to fan the flame.

Daddy had a lot of his mother in him that way, along
with inheriting her darker skin, strong jaw, and deep-set
brown eyes. But he had the height of my granddaddy,
Lemuel Herrington, who was 6'2" and skinny as a rail.
We called him Pappy and he and Little Emma made
quite a pair. Daddy was the oldest of sixteen children and
here I thought Pappy was a nice old man. Daddy grew
up in Bay Springs, Mississippi, and learned to revere his
parents at an early age. Pappy never let misbehavior go
unnoticed because he was a preaching man and cared
sincerely about making wrongs right.

Daddy's parents often travelled from their home up north to stay several weeks with each of their children every year. We couldn't wait for our turn for our grandparents to pack their trunks and come down to Arp for a month or more.

Pappy had a strong presence about him like my father. But unlike Daddy, Pappy knew the Bible backwards and forwards most of his life. He would gather all of the children around his chair and tell us things from Revelation about the Battle of Armageddon and all the frightening events that would happen to signal the end of the world. These stories about the horrible plagues on the earth made my hair stand up on end and kept me awake at night.

My mother's parents, Rufus and Emma Haire, were also originally from Bay Springs, but they were the exact opposite of Daddy's parents in some ways. They were not wealthy by any means, but they had more money than Daddy did so that made them seem rich to me. They rented out three big rooms on the top floor of their large home because it was too much space just for them. I remember playing with a boy named Joe Jr., a cousin who lived upstairs with his family for a time. Other than to say hello to Joe Jr., I was otherwise terrified to go up those creaky stairs to the upper floor.

The Haires were also strict. Staunch Christians and very conservative, they held a tight rein on their children growing up and were no different with their grandchildren. I was always scared to death of Grandmother Haire. She wore long, floor-length dresses that gave the appearance of a Victorian giant constantly towering over us disapprovingly.

At my mother's house, there was always something to eat and she was very generous with everyone. But at Grandmother Haire's home, everything was very prim and proper around mealtimes. Grandfather Haire sat straight as a board in his chair to recite the blessing and you'd just have to starve to death if you were still hungry after the meal because there was no such thing as a bedtime snack.

From a young age, I've always been pretty bold and willing to take a risk. Some risks I took worked out— some did not. One day I pretended to rest on top of a large trunk in Grandmother Haire's hallway until I saw her walk past me. Then I hopped up and raced into the kitchen to grab a biscuit out of the bread safe. She would have been happy to give me one if I had asked politely, but I was too intimidated by her to ask.

I sometimes wonder how my father felt around the Haire family when he was a young man and for the first time met the mother and father of the woman he loved.

✦

WHEN MY DAD LIVED in Bay Springs, there was nothing going on there for young men with any ambition. He dropped out of high school to go to work and was in his twenties when he and his two brothers decided to move to Texas to pick cotton. Uncle Jay, Uncle Albert, and my father worked their way south and eventually found jobs on Mother's family farm in Arp.

As fate would have it, my mother (who was six years younger than Daddy when they met) developed a crush on the handsome stranger who began working for her parents picking cotton. She liked the way he dressed and how he took such care with his appearance. She would wait all day for the chance to go outside in the late afternoons and swing on the front gate just when the young men were coming in from the fields. It wasn't long before my father noticed that the boss's daughter was a very beautiful young woman. They secretly began seeing each other and soon fell in love.

One day my mother confided to one of her older sisters, Aunt Ella, how much she loved my Daddy. Aunt Ella had a home of her own and allowed the couple to come there for rendezvous on her front porch where Mother and Daddy could safely sit and talk for hours. When my mother was finally eighteen, they made plans to spend the rest of their lives together, even if they had to run away to do it.

My dad was an honorable man and knew what he had to do. He had to tell Grandfather Haire that he loved his daughter so that he could have his blessing to marry her. But my grandfather would not hear one word of it. A worker marrying his daughter? He shamed my father and punished my mother for falling in love with someone whom he considered far beneath her class—a red-faced hillbilly, he called him.

I am sure that Grandfather Haire meant well, despite his strong response to my father's request to marry his daughter. He thought my mother's life would be over if she married my father. Grandmother Haire, however, could see that the young couple was truly in love. She even helped my mother and father hatch a plan to marry anyway. Aunt Ella bought the young couple two train tickets to Van Buren, Arkansas, where Minnie Louvina Haire became Mrs. William Lemuel Herrington before a justice of the peace. In the end, Mother and Daddy surprised everyone—even her father—because they stayed happily married over 60 years until my father's death.

However, that did not mean they had an easy time. My father never got over their rejection, and he was not even allowed to go to the house whenever Mother went to see her parents after they married. My grandfather made it clear that he did not want to see Daddy, and he was never welcome in their home. Even after we were born, nothing changed. Mother often went to my grandparents' house with us on Sunday afternoons for a family lunch. But Daddy was never invited to join.

It broke my heart whenever he had to drop us off at their house until we were ready for him to come get us to go home. I don't know where he went on Sunday afternoons by himself, but I believe this is one of the reasons why Daddy drank so heavily. He spent much of his life trying to cover the pain and deal with not measuring up to my grandfather's high standards.

My father was not one to cry easily, and I am much the

same way. One of the few times I saw my father shed tears was after we'd come home one Sunday from visiting my grandparents. These visits were hard on him, and it was hard on us to leave him behind all alone. I was excited to see him again and tell him about our afternoon, but my face fell when I noticed his eyes were watery from crying and bloodshot from alcohol. How he hated to be away from all of us. I am a pleaser and can hardly stand for anyone to hurt without trying to do something about it. I didn't know what else to do that day but to throw my arms around his waist and bury my head in his shirt, promising I'd never go off and leave him again.

To his credit, Grandfather Haire finally took Daddy into the family right before my grandfather died. Even he had to admit that my dad had turned out to be a faithful husband and good father to all of us—the very best.

Sometimes I think about all the years my Mother saw him hurting and all the weeks she spent away from him when he was out of town working. My mother had asked God to change her husband, and in God's perfect timing, my Daddy became a completely different man. All that Mother and Daddy went through to be together turned out to be worth it in the end.

My parents married for love. I wanted to marry for love, too, and would soon meet and date a man in the Service and marry him on the spot nineteen days later straight out of high school.

CHAPTER FOUR

# Girls in the Shipyard

"Can I really go?" I nearly squealed with excitement awaiting Daddy's answer to my question and I hoped he would say yes.

I was eighteen years old and still in school. Daddy and Mother were sitting across from me in the living room of our home. He had a stern look on his face and Mother seemed as if she might cry. I had the chance to join five other girlfriends from my high school who were going down to Houston for five months to volunteer at the Brown Shipbuilding Company during World War II.

When news of Pearl Harbor broke, men of every age in Arp volunteered to enlist immediately. Even my daddy tried to sign up because he wanted to help defend our country. It was too bad that the Army wouldn't take him, because he'd always said he could have killed the enemy with a brush broom. Our high school classrooms suddenly had empty desks as more of my classmates joined hundreds of thousands of young men from all over Texas who were being shipped overseas to fight. The women were doing their part, too. Following Al's example after he joined the Navy, when Jean graduated from nursing school she became a second lieutenant in the Army Nurses Corp to tend to wounded soldiers.

I was sixteen years old and sitting in a movie theater with my friends in December of 1941 when the lights suddenly came on and the movie reel stopped. We craned our necks and looked around trying to figure out what happened. The film probably broke, I thought. But then a man walked into the theater and announced that the Japanese had bombed Pearl Harbor. We were at war, he said!

Ever since that day I'd wanted to do something important for the war effort. And now this was my chance. The Navy needed several women volunteers to deliver orders and other important papers between offices at the shipyard. My girlfriends had already convinced their parents to let them go, and they were anxiously waiting for my parents to say I could join them.

I couldn't believe it when my parents finally agreed I could go. Daddy had had a long talk with the father of one of the girls. He must have decided I wouldn't be gone long enough to get in too much trouble down there. I jumped up and hugged Daddy's sun-tanned neck. His only rule was that I would come back after the five months were over and finish my senior year in school.

"Myrtle Louise, you are going to come back here and finish your education," Daddy said, his dark brown eyes nearly boring a hole in me. He used both of my names for extra emphasis.

"Yes, Daddy. I will," I said, my mind a million miles away, thinking about what I would pack.

Mother had married Daddy instead of going to college. And Daddy would have given anything if he could have finished high school instead of dropping out to go work. It was not surprising that education was very important to my parents. He wanted to make sure I graduated, and

I wanted to make sure I didn't disappoint him. But how was I to know in that moment that I'd never want to come home from Houston again?

I SOON BOARDED A train in Arp bound for Houston. The railway that had crisscrossed our town was now taking me far away to a big city I'd only heard about. The woman who ran the boarding house where we had arranged to stay took good care of us, and her concern for all of the girls set our parents at ease. All I cared about was that Ms. Gladys Crouch's home was on Main Street right where all the action was. It was a large two-story with a working fire escape on one side of the house. I knew it worked because I had to use it one time to climb in a window when I came home after curfew.

Ms. Crouch was a widow with funny quirks, including always setting a place for her deceased husband at the dinner table. My friends and I would trade glances at each other the first few times she did it, but we eventually got used to her ritual. We usually talked and laughed at dinner about the adventures of our day and passed around a bowl of spaghetti and baskets of the best rolls you ever ate. Everyone carefully rationed food during the war, including sugar, flour, coffee, and a list of other things. But Ms. Crouch could make the best meals from the limited items in her kitchen. She always followed dinner with a homemade pie or cake that was out of this world.

I had never imagined living in such a large home. It had to be even better than the Harmon house, I thought. There were three rooms for the six of us to share. Each room had its own bathroom, too. This came in handy in the mornings with six girls trying to get dressed for the day.

My entire home in Arp was three small rooms, and I'd somehow shared it with nine other people without issue. Sharing three rooms and three bathrooms with just six people now seemed absolutely luxurious. I soon began to wonder how I'd ever made do in the cramped space back home in East Texas.

The boys were fighting for freedom, and we girls were experiencing it for the first time. We were young and on our own. Plus, we were doing something vitally important for our country—all at the same time. We lived in a different time in our nation then. Everyone gladly did whatever they could on the home front to support the war. There was a great sense of unity that I'm afraid we've lost over the years.

When I was younger, we'd collected scrap metal for the military. My siblings and I rode in the wagon drawn by Nelly Bell, combing the back roads and countryside looking for tinfoil scraps, including the foil liners of cigarette packs. We rolled the foil into tight balls and hoist iron pieces onto the back of our wagon until we had enough to take to the railroad station for men to turn it into ammunition and guns.

Our entire community participated in scrap metal drives, and the pile at the station often grew so high that I couldn't peer over the top of it. In the early days of the war, I remember seeing train after train come through Arp with soldiers by the dozens hanging out of the windows and waving to us as the train made the last mile into the station. Sometimes Mother would let us bake cookies to take down to there to give to the grateful soldiers. Our church hosted several of them from nearby Camp Fannin in Tyler, and I didn't mind when Mother invited several of them over for lunch at our home.

Now that I was old enough to leave home and work

at the shipyard, I could do even more. The Navy kept us busy delivering bills of material from office to office every day. The shipyard gave me a bicycle to make my deliveries easier, and I would pedal between destinations with official paperwork safely tucked into a big woven basket fastened to my handlebars. We thought we looked awfully cute in our company-issued uniforms—especially our smart dark jackets.

My girlfriends and I met sailors by the dozens every week—boys from all over who were docked while their ship was being built or repaired. The sailors were very respectful of us, and I suspect that had a lot to do with our boss. He looked out for all of us with a keen eye for trouble. He may have had a talk with the Navy boys for all we knew, but they never one time got fresh with us. They liked to write their addresses in our autograph books, and of course we swore we'd write them all.

I did write many of them, as promised. I still have my autograph book, and as I turn the yellowed pages I sometimes wonder whatever happened to those brave young men with their whole lives ahead of them. Did they make it through the war, or were some of them killed in action? I'll never know, but the memories of their clean-cut, smiling faces are just as vivid as if it were yesterday.

I went out with several sailors—we all did. The time I had to use the fire escape to come in after curfew was after one such date. Mrs. Crouch had strict rules about no male visitors and she held us to an 11:00pm curfew. My roommate helped me crawl in through the window because the front door was already locked. All I had to do was picture my daddy's face if I'd gotten in trouble with one of those men—that was enough to scare me straight and head for home.

On one occasion, some sailors found out where the girls and I lived on Main Street. They pulled down the fire escape ladder and crawled up to our window and knocked. It nearly frightened us to death to open the yellow drapes and see those grinning sailors, their faces glued to the glass. Having soldiers over would not have worked for Mrs. Crouch—and it didn't work for us either. We closed the drapes in their faces and giggled nervously until they finally gave up and left.

One night at dinner soon after that night Mrs. Crouch dropped a hint that it might be time for us to start looking for another place to live. That woman knew everything. I think we had finally worn her out, six bubbly teenage girls living underfoot. We started looking for another house we could rent and shortly found one further away from Main Street in a nice neighborhood. The lady of the house was renting it out because she was living in Washington with her husband who was also in the Service.

With Mrs. Crouch's blessing, and not a minute too soon, we packed up our things and moved to the new house all by ourselves. The small house was also on the bus line, and we could walk to the corner to take the bus to the shipyard. After a while, one of my girlfriends got a little motorbike to ride to work. She tried to talk me into riding on the back of it with her, but I hopped right off the first time we rode fifty feet together. I couldn't figure out how to balance, shifting my weight left and right to keep us upright. It wasn't like riding Nelly Bell at all, and I was afraid I would tump us over on the street and kill us both.

Like my mother and father, I would never have the opportunity to go to college. This was my college experience in a lot of ways, only cheaper. None of us had been away from Arp and our families for any extended period of time. It was fun to learn how to run a household, and we took turns cooking our meals and cleaning.

We all worked hard during the week and by the time the weekend rolled around, we would almost all have dates. I no longer minded wearing make-up by then. My roommates and I had a ritual of spending a good bit of time every weekend doing our hair and sharing the bathroom mirror while we got ready to go out.

I went on my share of blind dates. One and only one of those blind dates was with an Army man. Big mistake. Where the sailors had always been respectful and courteous, I had to get away from that pushy Army man and walk to a payphone to call the girls to come get me. They said, "Lou, you stay right there and wait for us." We all walked home together and piled into one bed so I could tell them my story. I was pretty shaken, but we all ended up laughing in the end and everything was alright once again. I've learned in life that there are friends who eat your heart up and leave you with nothing. And then there are friends who give you more heart. Those girls were those kinds of friends to me.

I wasn't the only one who'd had a bad experience on a date. I'll never forget when another one of the girls agreed to go out on a first date with a young man she wasn't too sure about. "Just whistle, and we'll come running if you need us," we assured her. Sure enough, she needed us to rescue her before she'd even gotten down the street. All five of us went tearing out of the house at her signal and ran out into the yard. Only there was a clothesline that I didn't see. We usually had fresh laundry hanging on it, but this time it was picked clean. The line caught me at the neck and flung me down to the ground so quickly that my head was spinning and I saw stars. My girlfriends and I got so tickled that I thought we would never stop laughing may have even wet our pants. That was some night.

IN SOME WAYS, I wanted this exciting experience in Houston to go on forever. I even halfway convinced myself that maybe it could. But things changed as the war progressed. America and her allies were winning, and a final victory looked like it was finally in our grasp. Over time not as many personnel were needed at the shipyard because they weren't sending as many ships into battle. One of the girls eventually went back to Arp, and the rest of us wondered who would be the next to go home. My parents called from time to time, and we talked about when I might return home to Arp.

"I don't want to leave," I told them flat out. "But I'll do whatever you really want me to do," I always added.

But when it came down to it, I didn't really mean that. I didn't want to finish school. I wanted to finish the war. So I quietly planned to stay on as long as possible and find more work that I could do for the Navy. Surely there was something I could do.

After a full afternoon at work one day I parked my bicycle in my typical spot at the shipyard and walked out of the gate to catch the bus to go home. I was meeting my girlfriends at the house for dinner as usual. I was totally caught up in my thoughts about the evening ahead when a strong male hand caught me by the arm and turned me around. Daddy. When my eyes met his, I knew I'd just spent my last day in the shipyard.

I went back to Arp with him on the first train out of Houston. I didn't know it then, but my time as a footloose and fancy-free teenager was coming to an important crossroad. Within a few months, my life would dramatically and unexpectedly change forever.

## CHAPTER FIVE

# War, Heartbreak, and Marriage

One of the brave young men from Arp who served in World War II was named Hubert. We dated a little in high school, and I consider him my first love from the time I was sixteen years old. He would call me and we'd meet up by the big shade tree in the yard so he could take me to church in his family's pickup. Any time I tried slipping away with

Hubert, thinking we were all alone, we'd inevitably run into Daddy one way or another. That man seemed to be everywhere at once. He knew where I was going before I'd even gotten there!

One night I jumped in Hubert's pickup to go to church, but we ended up going for a little drive instead. The main part of the Arp community was two square miles at the time so we could not go far. We were holding hands going down the road and having a good time when I suddenly saw the bright glow of headlights behind us. They came closer and closer. It was Daddy! I hit the floorboard with a thud and whispered to Hubert, "Drive to the church quick! It's my daddy behind us!" Hubert got us to church, but I got in trouble once again. I'll never forget the last time I snuck out of my house to see Hubert. There was a mesh screen on the window of the bedroom that Jean and I shared, and I got pretty good at lifting it up and slipping out unnoticed. Hubert would meet me by the big tree in our yard and off we'd go. That last night I'd had a fun time with Hubert and as I was crawling back in the window, I reached for the string that hung down from the single lightbulb in our room. Instead of a string, my hand met up with Daddy's face!

"I'll tend to you tomorrow," he said as I tumbled over the window frame and onto the floor of my room. Jean just laughed into her pillow, but I was miserable.

"Daddy! Whip me now!" I pleaded, brushing off my knees as I stood up. But it was too late. He was gone. It was a sleepless night that dragged on forever until the morning sun finally came streaking through our window. Daddy could really lay it on you.

We never had a car in our family other than the old pickup Daddy drove, and I was a teenager before we had a telephone in our home. But almost everyone had a radio in the living room to tune in to the latest reports on the war. Texas was still very rural and many families were finally coming out of the Depression when the war began. Most Texans lived on farms and ranches surrounding small towns like mine. Ordinarily, the boys like the ones I went to school with would grow up in the house where they were born, join their dad working in whatever job he did, marry, and raise their family just as their parents had done and their parents before them. But the war would change all that. The war changed everything.

Hubert was soon off fighting a war that we were all convinced the USA would eventually win. Almost every family's mailbox brought regular news to our tiny community from sons, fathers, and brothers who were serving across the ocean thousands of miles away. Soldiers often kept their spirits up by writing home and making big plans for their lives when they returned. Hubert was no exception. He and I corresponded back and forth while he was away. In one of his letters Hubert confessed that he had marriage in mind when he was finally free to come home!

But I was very young and not as confident that we shared the same plans for our future since Hubert would be gone several years. Time, I decided, would just have to tell.

I SOON FOUND MYSELF thinking that as much as I cared for Hubert, I was also in love with several other boys along the way. And like most typical teenage girl, my feelings changed from week to week. My girlfriends and I often rode our bicycles to Troup (another small town just a few miles away) to be around those good-looking Troup boys. Robert and I were just friends, but we loved to dance together. My friend Pete and I were never in love but we were very much "in like." I had many guy friends like them, but my best guy friend was Billy Beard. If neither of us had a date, we'd go together to parties and dance the night away.

He is still part of so many of my best memories. We kept in touch after we grew up and remained friends. When he got very ill, I went to see him and brought him a cake I had baked. He must have known he did not have long because he joked, "Wonder if I'll get to eat it all?" We spent some time trading stories until I could see in his eyes that he was tired. He died three days later.

We had to go to our friends' houses if we wanted to dance on the weekends because Arp took care of our school gym as if it were a diamond. Nobody was going to jitterbug on it if they had their way. Camp Fannin hosted a few dances for the soldiers, and when I was older my girlfriends and I took a bus from Arp to the camp and danced. Sometimes the Camp Fannin soldiers took us to a couple of other places in Tyler where young people could dance.

I was in it strictly for fun, but one night some boys told us they were taking us to a dance and they pulled up in a Tyler hotel parking lot instead. Daddy would kill me if he knew where I was, and I was already nervous about what these boys had in mind. So I got another ride out of there quickly. I learned later that one girl I knew got pregnant and had to get married. No one talked about that happening in those days. In our small town, three girls in my high school got pregnant, and one even killed herself after having her baby.

I looked forward to Friday night football games and spent my time having all the fun a high school girl could have. My friends and I were on the cheer squad, and we would run up and down the sidelines pulling for the Arp Tigers to win. We cheered our hearts out every Friday night until we were hoarse on Saturday morning. I don't have a musical bone in my body, but I learned to play the snare drum in high school. Our school was so small that the students didn't have to try out for anything. The band director just asked one day if I'd like to play the snare drum and I said I'd give it a try.

With the exception of the few months I spent away in the shipyard, I had a very typical American high school experience. When I reluctantly returned from the shipyard to finish my senior year, I did not expect much else to happen. I believed that I'd had my best experiences and now that was over. I would just finish out the year to make my parents happy and go from there. But that's when one special young man came into my life.

Martin Eugene Pettis was the older brother of a friend of mine. He fascinated me because he was an Army man serving overseas as a sergeant. I hung on every word as he spun tales of his adventures when he was home on furlough during my senior year. He had stormed the beaches of Normandy and had once delivered a baby on the side of the road. He was truly a man of the world to a naïve girl who had barely been beyond the borders of Arp. I fell head over heels in love with his Southern charm and Army crewcut. When Gene asked me one night to marry him just nineteen days after we met, I agreed without hesitation. We secretly planned our wedding day and did not tell my parents until the last minute because we were rightfully afraid of what they might say.

I graduated from high school, went to prom, and got married the next day. There are not too many other people I know who can say their fiancé was also their prom date. I discovered at prom that evening to my great disappointment that Gene did not like to dance—

the first of many discoveries I'd make about my soon-to-be husband. I think I was born dancing, I love it to this day very much. I have fond memories of my friends and I throwing a barn dance at our home when I was in junior high. We stacked up hay bales for kids to sit on and kept the Victrola busy playing records all night. I could dance until my feet absolutely hurt. On the other hand, Gene preferred to watch rather than venture out on the dance floor. Still, I was proud to introduce him to all my friends and my teachers that night. I dreamed of our beautiful wedding that night as we sat at some small tables and watched everyone having a good time.

ONE DAY NOT LONG after I'd been married, I heard the doorbell ring at my mother's house. Standing at the front door with a huge grin on his face was a soldier. It was Hubert! He was home from the war. Before I could speak, he swept me up in his arms and was about to plant a big kiss on me when I pushed him away and slid out of his embrace.

"Oh, Hubert," I said, smoothing my hair and dress nervously. "You can't do that. I'm married."

For a minute he just stood there smiling dumbstruck, as if what I'd said did not even register with him. Then his face fell, and I felt so sorry for him as I watched all his plans come to an abrupt end.

"Let's talk a minute," I said and offered him a seat on our front porch.

I told him that Gene and I had been married for only a few months. It had all happened so suddenly, I told him, that there had been no time to explain. I promised him that it was not his fault. I had simply fallen in love with someone else and we were happy together. I could hear Gene in the house talking with Mother and silently prayed that he would not come out on the porch looking for me. Hubert and I parted ways and I walked back in the house to join my family at the table. I didn't say a word to anyone.

Several decades later I was thinking about this experience and remembered that Hubert had sent me money for an engagement ring in one of his many letters. As a young girl with many potential suitors ahead of me (so I thought), I eventually spent the money on something else while Hubert was still overseas. I was in my eighties when the memories surrounding Hubert's money came to mind.

Gene had been gone a long time by then, and the war years seemed as if they were another lifetime ago. But I began to feel so guilty that I had spent that money on myself. I couldn't sleep at night. I had not been in touch with Hubert since that time and wasn't even sure he was still alive. I turned to my younger sister Ellen to see if she could find Hubert so that I could make it right. Ellen could find anybody in the world long before the Internet arrived on the scene! It took her a while to search through her contacts and connections, but she finally found Hubert living in a small town in Texas.

Ellen gave me Hubert's phone number and I called him the next day. His wife answered the phone. I explained that Hubert and I had been friends in Arp way back during the war and that he had given me some money one time that I wanted to repay.

"Please let me give it back to him," I asked.

She just laughed and said, "You'll have to tell Hubert this story. He'll get a kick out of it."

I wasn't so sure that was exactly how he would react. After all, I thought I'd broken his heart. But he came on the phone and Hubert said he'd forgotten all about the money. It was a while before he finally agreed (after much groveling on my part) to let me mail him a check.

I never felt so good about writing a check as I did that day to get it off my conscience. I've always tried to keep short accounts with people—I don't like to have things hanging over my head. I will quickly say I'm sorry when I am wrong (and sometimes even when I'm not). If I feel that I can do something to make a situation right, I try to act right away and not put it off. This was one situation that I'd put off for more than half my life. But one thing life has taught me is that it's never too late to try to set things right with people—no matter how long it's been.

◈

ONE OF THE REASONS why Gene and I married so quickly was that he was going back overseas to rejoin his unit shortly after our wedding. We were young, but we were both old enough to know better than to rush to the altar. Still, we went headlong into our future together because we were in love. When Gene and I finally met with Mother and Daddy at the kitchen table and explained to them that we loved each other and that we were getting married the next day, I thought I'd cry my eyes out. Mother had to talk Daddy down initially because he did not like the idea at all. I was the first of his children to get married and Daddy wasn't one bit ready to let me go. Of course, I didn't know it then, but I found out much later as an adult that my father could relate to our situation much more than he'd let on that day at the kitchen table. He'd also hatched a secret plan to marry my mother when they had no business getting married. It turns out that Daddy and I were more alike in that moment than he'd wanted to admit. I could only hope that things would turn out half as well for us as they had for my parents.

## CHAPTER SIX

# Young and Married

My parents eventually gave us their blessing that day, and Mother and I moved on to talking about more important things like what I would wear to my wedding. My only choice was to wear the beautiful and frilly short pink dress she'd already bought me for my high school graduation ceremony—an event that would take place only a few hours later that afternoon. It was the perfect dress and it was as beautiful at graduation as it was at the wedding.

On Saturday morning, as planned, Gene and I went looking for my pastor to see if he could marry us. Only he wasn't in the church. When we found him, he was working underneath his pier-and-beam house, covered from head to toe in dirt. He brushed himself off, shook Gene's hand, and tried not to look shocked when we told him our plans. We talked him into performing the ceremony for us and by the end of the day I was Mrs. Gene Pettis. We drove south a few hours from Arp to Groveton for a short three-night honeymoon at a hotel and moved in with my parents for a few weeks before Gene would leave for the Pacific.

The first night we were together after we married, I cried for the next three days. Mother had always taught me that sex was a sin. We were taught that all down the line, and she'd laid the idea pretty thick on each one of her children. It was a strange three weeks living under my parents' roof after Gene and I returned from our honeymoon. I couldn't help wondering what Mother and Daddy thought about us being together as husband and wife, but Gene was patient with me and with my other family members who were always underfoot. Gene and I would sometimes sneak off holding hands for a walk in the woods just to be alone for a short time before someone would discover us.

Being a newlywed was like being dropped off on another planet. No one prepared young women like me for marriage back then—overnight you had to get used to what a husband wanted to do, how he liked his clothes, and how he liked his food. To tell the truth, it was a relief when we took Gene to the train station to report for duty. But I teared up as I kissed him goodbye, not sure when he would return, if ever. Victory still seemed certain, but the war was far from over because Japan was still a genuine threat to the United States, and that's where Gene was headed.

I thought Gene's absence would give me time to get used to the idea of being married. But living at home with my mom and dad again made me quickly resume my old life. Part of me desperately wanted to go back to my routine of being with my friends and going out dancing every night until the day Gene came home. After all, who knew when that day would be? I could be alone a long time. I missed my husband as much as a young new bride could, but I was also very happy to be the apple of my Daddy's eye again.

To my surprise, I got a letter in the mail from Gene a short time later saying he was coming home to stay.

The Army had discharged him. Our whole country celebrated VE Day on May 8, 1945, after the Germans surrendered. The war was over. And so was playtime. I remember reading those lines in his letter over and over. "I'm coming home for good," Gene had written. I was a mess. I was glad that he was coming home, but I felt so guilty that I wasn't happier about this news.

It took Gene a while to ship back to the United States, and the days seemed very long as I waited for his return. The afternoon he was to arrive in Arp by train, I dressed up and carefully did my hair, but I was a nervous wreck. My entire family went to the station with me to welcome him home, and we leaned over every few minutes to look down the tracks and see if we could watch the engine pulling into view. When I saw the train come in and watched Gene step off the car in his United States military uniform, that's all it took. He was mine once more. I ran into his arms, kissed him, and we fell in love all over again. But we had many hard days ahead of us.

GENE AND I LIVED in Arp in my parents' home at first and slowly grew more comfortable living together as a married couple—this time for more than a few weeks. Although my parents had not wanted me to marry so young (and so quickly), they eventually came to love Gene.

Like me, he was also the first child in his family to get married. They were from Overton. His father was a minister and they had a large family like mine with several brothers and sisters. They were all very musical and played in a family band. His father could make the violin strings sound heavenly. They had been performing at bars and honky tonks throughout East Texas for years and continued performing together after Gene married. I often stayed home when they played these gigs. It seemed crazy to me to go out so late all the time to these places. Gene had almost been engaged to another girl before we married, and sometimes I feared that he might go back to her (or someone else) if he ever got tired of me. Looking back, I can see how I was young and spoiled, and I'm sure he saw that too.

After a year, Gene eventually decided to go to school in Dallas since the Army would pay for it. I did not want to leave my family in Arp, but I was glad in some ways for us to get away and start fresh in another city. When we moved, we lived in the basement of an apartment home near the Oak Lawn area of Dallas. Life changed for us as a couple then because we were finally on our own completely. I even got my first real job working for my uncle at the Toddle House. This chain was a small diner with counter service only and a long row of stools.

I worked nights, which was great because I discovered that it was the best time to earn tips from people who went to big parties and came in half-drunk for a bite to eat afterwards. My face was so tired from smiling at the end of every shift. But my best customers often left me ten and twenty-dollar tips—a lot of money just for a tip and a whole lot of money back then. One winter, Dallas had a terrible ice storm and it took me longer than usual to get to work. I was behind the counter getting ready for the day when I saw Johnson, a man I worked with, hurrying up the sidewalk. He was all bundled up in his wool coat when he slipped on the ice by the front door and sailed headlong past all the windows right into the azalea bushes. "I could have been killed!" he huffed as I bent over laughing at him, but he was eventually smiling too.

Along with Johnson, I also remember George and Lucinda who worked in the back at the Toddle House. They were quite the characters. Lucinda would tell us wild tales, including the time that she went to "high-five." This was her name for the county jail. I sat wide-eyed as she told us how she had nearly killed her boyfriend with a pistol the night that the police had arrested her. George usually came by to say goodnight whenever he was leaving his shift. More than once he'd tuck a couple of pounds of wrapped bacon in his shirt just to see if I would notice. "I best be going, Miss Lou," he'd tell me and make his way toward the door. But I'd tap his shirt and say sweetly, "George, you're not going anywhere with all that bacon, are you?" And he would grin and say, "No ma'am. I was just keeping it warm."

I was making a good living for the first time in my life when we lived in Dallas. Like many women, I enjoyed the feeling of having financial security. When I finally put enough money aside, I walked into a store that had a beautiful black sweater in the display window and bought it. It was the most expensive gift I'd ever purchased for myself. I'd passed by that store window a hundred times for months thinking about that sweater and reminding myself of what I used to say when I was young: "This is just today. Tomorrow I will be something else." When I looked in the mirror wearing my new black sweater, I felt like someone else alright—a grown up. Instead of a kid, I saw a secure and confident young woman looking back at me. To me, that sweater was not just a piece of clothing. It represented something much more. I'd worked hard for something that I wanted, and I kept that sweater for years even after it became too old and frayed to wear anymore.

WHEN I GOT PREGNANT with our first child, I was thrilled to pieces to become a mother. Most of all, I wanted to be with my mama. I moved back to Arp to prepare for the birth while Gene planned to finish up school in Dallas. But then he decided to go in another direction. He quit school and began working with my dad on a pipeline in Houston.

An older man, Gene knew a lot about life that I didn't—most of which he learned during the four years he served overseas. Anything I knew about being a woman I learned from my mother. I never realized how important those lessons were until I needed to draw on them. When I was a girl, my mother and I talked about life as we went along, and I learned many things from watching her example. When I was pregnant, we talked even more. I'd sit on the front porch in the late afternoons shelling peas and drinking glasses of iced tea. She went over everything I needed to do to get ready to have the baby. Since she'd given birth seven times, I considered my mother an expert. However, I was green as a fig and wondered what kind of mother I'd be.

Whenever I pictured holding my newborn baby, rocking on our front porch with Mother and Daddy and all my family around me, I felt better about the future. I missed Gene and wanted him to come home from being gone so long on jobs with Daddy. It was time for us to have a family of our own.

I gave birth to a son we named Richard in the hospital in the nearby town of Jacksonville after spending several tough days in labor. Becoming a mother changed me in an instant. I never knew how much I could love someone until I had my first child. I thought Richard was the cutest thing on two feet. Just as I had imagined I'd do one day, Gene and I were now raising a family in Arp. Once more we lived with my parents, and we enjoyed it very much. We lived with them until we saved enough money to move to our own home in the Hollywood Edition of my little town. This little patch of property was not quite the real Hollywood Hills and was really just a shotgun style house with a nook on the side. But it was all ours, and I thought I'd died and gone to heaven. As a new mother, it was comforting to me to be in familiar surroundings. I cooked bacon and eggs most mornings before Gene went to work and happily contented myself with my new baby. Mother and Daddy were wild about their first grandchild and spoiled him with love every minute of every day.

I don't know why, but throughout my life I have spent considerable time daydreaming and quietly thinking and praying about what I wanted to happen next. I usually enjoyed being wherever I was—but I was always curious about what was down the road and around the corner. This time was no different. I began dreaming of raising all of our children exactly where and how I'd grown up, enjoying the safety and security that a small town can afford. My parents certainly didn't want us going anywhere either now that they had a grandchild. To me our future seemed settled, but that conclusion was as far from the truth as it could get.

GENE CAME HOME ONE day and told me he'd taken a new job with an oil company out in West Texas. I stared at him, not certain of what he'd said. West Texas? I had barely been outside of East Texas, much less hundreds of miles and many hours away in that dry, flat part of Texas that was closer to Arizona and New Mexico than the green pastures I loved. But he'd already made the decision, so that was that. When the three of us packed up and moved to the small town of Odessa, I thought Gene had brought me to the very ends of the earth. We were more than half a day's drive from my family in Arp and we lived in very primitive conditions for the first few months we were there. Everyone who was trying to get in on the oil boom out west was living shoulder to shoulder in makeshift homes, rickety trailers, and whatever else they could find. We knew a man who even slept in the nose of an old cargo plane for a while. The bright lights of the oil derricks stayed on twenty-four hours a day while men like my husband worked day and night to pump oil out of the ground.

It was something akin to living in the Wild West. Or during the Gold Rush of California. It was every man for himself and everyone was just trying to cash in on the opportunities there. The wind blew constantly in Odessa, driving clouds of dust and fine sand everywhere. The first big dust storm nearly cured me forever of remaining out there. One minute the sun was shining and the next minute the entire sky was black as night. When the storm was over, we had to shovel sand out of our driveway like snow just to back up the car into the street. I stayed in Odessa about five days the first week we moved there and came straight home to Arp!

My parents made me go back. But this became the routine. I'd stay four or five days, then I'd take the baby with me and come home again. I drove two-lane highways all the way from Odessa to Arp in the Ford Fairlane 500 I'd bought with the money I'd earned at the Toddle House. After going back and forth like this

a while, Mother finally sat me down and told me that
I needed to stay out there and make a go of it with my
husband.

I made myself a promise—if I stayed in Odessa, I was
not going to stay at home missing my parents and being
bored to death. I decided to get a job to take me out
of the house and so I could meet people. There was a
popular drive-in called the Speedway near our home.
One day I put Richard in the stroller and walked up there
to ask for a job. I told the boss about all my experience
as a short-order cook, and he hired me on the spot. I
was to come to the Speedway the next day and start
working the fountain where we served sodas, ice cream,
and shakes. I didn't have to wear a uniform, just a white
apron over my clothes. The worst job was washing all
the dirty dishes, but I didn't even mind that because I'd
grown up washing twelve people's dishes several times a
day.

I could do it all—cook, clean, work the fountain, and
be a car hop bringing out orders. Many nights, I was
flipping burgers until one in the morning and having a
great time doing it, too. Sometimes I'd play a joke on my
friends and sneak the paper liner from the meat patty
into their burger and watch from the window as they

took a big bite! The Speedway drew all kinds of people from all the little towns surrounding Odessa. On the weekends the boys would take their girls there. They'd buy their dates something cheap like a glass of soda, then take them home and return later for a malted and a burger with the boys! The Speedway often had live music, including a little-known singer who was living in Odessa named Roy. He was the West Texas Elvis, and I have a picture of me with my arms around him at the Speedway before he became the famous singer Roy Orbison.

I worked my way up in the business over the next few years, serving, cooking, and working some in the back office. I took Richard with me and made a little pallet for him in the corner so I could keep an eye on him. I had to watch out for him because I knew he'd end up on the roof of the Speedway when he learned to walk. One day the boss decided to let me partner with him in a fountain drink operation that he started in a warehouse in the back of the drive-in. I lifted fifty-pound bags of sugar on my shoulder to make the syrup using his special recipe. His job was to deliver the concoction to various customers. On the weekends when we were extra busy at the Speedway, I still enjoyed stepping in to help cook with an older lady we'd hired named Annie. Customers would park two and sometimes three rows deep all the way around the building. Annie and I would be so busy at the grill that several hours would pass before I could even look up.

The only thing Gene and I could afford when we first moved to Odessa was a small trailer. The cold wind blew through every crack and crevice in that silver bullet, and our baby's wet diapers would stick to the floor in the winter like frozen ice cubes! We had been married four years by the time we had Richard, which was a surprise to the town gossip in Arp who had predicted I was pregnant when I married Gene after high school. Mrs. Husson had to eat her words when I saw her back in Arp one day while visiting my parents with our three-year-old son. "Guess what?" I told her. "That baby that I was pregnant with when I got married is finally here!" That was the first and last time I'd ever seen Mrs. Husson speechless.

When we had saved enough money, the three of us moved from the trailer into the other half of a duplex in Odessa. The bathrooms were located outside in a common area shared by other duplexes, but this home was a great improvement over the trailer. The sweetest people named Honey and Bob owned the duplex and rented it to us. They worshiped our blonde-haired little boy. I soon learned that their own child had died of cancer, and it was no surprise that they grew to love Richard as if he were their son. Honey was a little woman, but Bob was probably six-foot-eight and never hesitated to drop to the ground and roll around in the backyard playing with Richard. They were godsends to us, and we were so thankful for their friendship. I also got involved in our church at Second Baptist in Odessa and became close with several women there, too.

It was still difficult to call Odessa home, however. I will never forget living through my first hail storm when baseball-sized hail rained down on us and beat the screens off the windows. When it was all over, broken glass was everywhere and jagged balls of ice were stacked nearly a foot high in the backyard. I'd stood stock still in the doorway during the storm, praying and thinking that the Tribulation that Pappy had warned us about as kids had finally started—in Odessa of all places.

In those moments I resented Gene for dragging us out there. I longed to be back in East Texas again, instead of staring out the window at a flat, brown landscape and wondering how in the world I ever ended up out there. Gene and I were both headstrong, and whenever we got crossways with each other we fought like brother and sister. I called him by his full name, Martin Eugene, whenever I was really upset. Some of those times are funny when I look back, like when I followed Gene outside on his way to the bathroom while we were arguing and threw a batch of bread dough at him. I missed his head when he ducked, but the dough landed in the "slop jar"—what we called the toilet. The next day, the yeast had risen to the lid of the toilet seat!

Motherhood was wonderful but stressful at the same time. Richard's bed was often the backseat of my car on the way to and from work, and he had to share my attention with my job. Gene and I were both working to make ends meet, and there did not seem to be enough hours in the day. We drove one time to Mississippi to see family and had carefully laid Richard's clothes in the backseat beside him near the window. When we got to Mississippi, Gene and I discovered that Richard had dropped every piece of his clothing out the window all along the way between Texas and Mississippi. Even his shoes! We had to go to a store and buy more clothes for him just to have something to wear.

By the time he was old enough to crawl, our son was

into everything. A perfect day was one when I would not have to turn to the police for help. But then again, I have to admit that I was an inexperienced mother myself.

When Richard was four years old, he got into his dad's wallet after Gene had cashed his paycheck. When we weren't looking, Richard went out the window in our duplex with the wallet, and we suddenly couldn't find him anywhere. The police eventually found him outside a store on a busy street waiting for the doors to open so he could buy something with Gene's money! I felt like a terrible mother, and Richard was disappointed that he didn't get to shop for anything.

One time I caught him taking rubber bands from my office at the Speedway, and that set me off. To teach him a lesson, I drove him to the police station and left him there. When I came back two hours later, he was sitting in the middle of all the policemen on top of one of their desks, drinking a Coke and having a great time. He can still get a whole room laughing telling stories. God is good because Richard survived his childhood and grew up to be a wonderful husband, father, and Sunday school teacher. He and I went through so much together and we're still very close.

One time my sister Ann and a childhood friend of hers

came to stay with us in Odessa for about two months. Our tiny duplex had a kitchen and dining area and a bedroom. We set up roll-away beds in the kitchen for the girls. We also covered the tops of all our beds with sheets during the day because that darn wind would blow dust over everything. It even made its way through the light switches and made tiny piles of fine dust on the floor underneath the switch plates.

I put Ann and Gwendolyn to work at the Speedway as car hops. They were so young and darling, flashing their big smiles at all the young men and getting big tips. They made more money in those two months than they'd seen in their whole lives. With her beautiful blonde hair, I had to beat the boys off my baby sister.

Over time, I started to feel more at home in Odessa. When we were able to move from the duplex to a small house with two bedrooms and a dining room, we thought we had it made. I was working more in the office at the Speedway now and helping run the business side of the operation. I had five girls who worked for me and they were all angels.

Gene and I had worked through several of the issues that a lot of young married couples have, and things were finally coming together for us. We learned to relax and laugh a lot more as life got easier. We hunted for fun whenever we visited Mother and Daddy in Arp— shooting pears off trees and the occasional bird or squirrel. Gene pretended to have a fit when his wife turned out to be a better shot with a rifle than he was! He played tricks on me and I usually got him back— with interest—as quickly as I could. One time I walked outside to get in my Ford Fairlane and discovered Gene had painted my pretty white sidewalls pink!

I made friends with the wives of some of Gene's co-workers and we went out as couples. My girlfriends and I would sometimes make special lunches for our husbands and bring them out to the oil rig. I remember we'd asked one of the girls to make a lemon pie to take with us one day. Times were tight. She was worried about all the money it'd cost her to make it. We carefully laid her pie on the dash of the car behind the backseat because she didn't want anything to happen to it. On the way to the rig, we had to slam on the brakes and that whole pie went flying forward! It ruined the pie—and ruined her day at the same time—but the rest of us had a good laugh telling the boys what had happened to dessert.

One day I woke up with the worst pain in my side. I could hardly walk, and it was all I could do to drag my left leg behind me. Something was seriously wrong and I was scared. Gene rushed me to the hospital, and I learned that I had developed kidney stones. They admitted me to the hospital immediately because I was very, very sick. This illness threw me off kilter because up to this point nothing had ever slowed me down. I was born busy and honestly didn't know how to rest and take it easy. But now in the hospital I was in such agony that at one point I was not even sure I would make it. When I gave birth to my son, it had not hurt nearly this much.

To make matters worse, there were no doctors who specialized in kidneys out in Odessa. The hospital finally found a doctor who came all the way up from Houston just to perform my surgery. My parents hopped in the car and drove to Odessa to help Gene take care of Richard while he worked and I recovered from my operation. All of my life, Mother was always there to help me.

The doctors would not allow me to have any visitors. I could only look out the window of my hospital room at my little boy and my parents waving at me in the yard down below. I cried when I saw them. I had to get better, I told the Lord. I could not die so young and leave Gene with our only son to raise all alone without me. I prayed earnestly that God would heal me so that I could be with my family again. And He did.

After I was strong enough to resume a busy schedule of work and motherhood, Gene and I began attending the Methodist church in town and made several friends there, too. One day I decided I wanted to be baptized in that church. I'd been baptized when I was younger, but I was an adult now. I felt the need to be cleansed, as if to make sure that any trouble in the past was far behind me.

Gene and I had been married ten years at that point and had been talking for some time about the day when we'd finally save enough to move into our dream home. We eventually designed and built the home ourselves, and I was looking forward to starting a fresh chapter there as a family. We'd been living there less than a year and had just finished furnishing each room just the way we wanted when tragedy struck. It's been more than sixty years since his death, and I still put flowers on Gene's grave.

## CHAPTER SEVEN

# Tragedy and Coming Home

The day that forever altered all of our lives started out like any other summer day. Gene had gone to Dallas on business and Richard was at church for Vacation Bible School. I was standing at the window on the morning of June 8, 1956, when I saw a couple from church coming up our walkway and they were crying. I immediately thought, "Oh no, something has happened to my baby." I ran out the front door and learned that it wasn't Richard who was hurt. It was Gene. He had spent the previous night in Dallas with my sisters Ann and Ellen. Evidently, he must have stayed up late in the evening because he fell asleep at the wheel on his way home to Odessa early the next morning on Highway 31 outside Athens. Two men who witnessed the crash said that our car was practically flying when it hit the first tree and bounced from one side of a culvert to the other. Gene was killed instantly just shy of his 37th birthday.

I was in a daze after I heard the news. I had to go home to Arp. I slowly and deliberately gathered enough clothes for myself and Richard into a suitcase, unable to think of anything at all. We had planned to go on our first family vacation in Florida later that summer. I packed some of the new clothes I'd bought Richard especially for the trip. I even packed some of Gene's new shirts as well. Part of me knew he would never have a chance to wear them, but the other part of me couldn't bear to leave his new clothes behind.

I was in shock and it had not yet hit me that Gene was dead. Forever. I would never talk to him again. I locked our house with my key and got in the car for the long ride back to East Texas. Hours passed and I did not know how I'd gotten from one town to the next. I had no recollection that I'd been driving for hundreds of miles. I was lost in my thoughts and memories. When I arrived at the Ft. Worth city limits, I was shocked back into reality when a policeman stopped me for speeding. That was the last thing I needed, but after I explained the situation, he agreed to let me go on my way without giving me a ticket.

I did not have any time to prepare myself for the funeral because it took so long to get home to Arp. By the time I arrived, Gene's body was already at the Overton funeral home and I went there right away for the viewing. It was awful. Completely exhausted, I collapsed in my parents' arms. Our young son would grow up without his father. I was now a widow. And I was alone and living hundreds of miles away from my family.

Before the funeral, I insisted on driving to the crash site outside Athens to look for some of Gene's belongings that had been scattered by the roadside. The funeral was heartbreaking and we buried my husband in Mason Cemetery in Arp.

I returned to Odessa with Mother a short while later. My church and other friends were so good to me, but

I already felt as if I no longer belonged there. Gene happened to have enough insurance to pay off the house, our two cars, and even the new refrigerator we had just bought. I knew that I could not stay in Odessa by myself and raise Richard. I hated to leave my job, the young girls who worked for me, and all the friends I'd made. But everything in me wanted to go home to East Texas where I belonged.

I would have to find a good job to support myself, and opportunities were slim for a young single mother in Arp. So I decided to move to Tyler where I would have a better chance of making it on my own. When life hits you hard, you have to gather what is left, hold it close, and move on. That you can do. You must do it. You can ask for God to give you strength to do it.

My mother and daddy were still living in Arp, and I asked them for a big favor. I wanted them to live with me temporarily in Tyler until I could get on my feet. I took some of the cash I'd saved and bought a small three-bedroom house on Woodhaven on the east side of Tyler. I remember the house payments were ninety-nine dollars a month. It was a lot to ask of my parents to come be with me, but they were glad to do whatever they could so I wouldn't be alone. They felt sorry for

Richard growing up without his father, and they wanted to be near their grandson. Dad was working in Kilgore at the time as a pipe-fitter and drove the thirty-minute commute every week.

Gene was the first sibling in his family to die, and as difficult as his sudden death had been on me, it overwhelmed his parents to the point of being inconsolable. Within ten months of his passing, they were both dead. I believe his father died of a broken heart. Gene's mother developed cancer. Near her death, I went to see her. When I held her in my arms, I felt her chest as hard as rocks against my own chest. Concerned, I held her away from me and asked, "What is this?"

She said softly, "Oh, it's nothing." Even though she was suffering, she told no one about her illness until it was too late. She died a short time later and they buried her next to her husband.

Like Gene's parents, there were times when I did not think I could make it out of the pain either. For the first year, I didn't go out anywhere. I didn't see anyone. I just tried to breathe and put one foot in front of the other each day. I would wake up and think, "I just can't do it again today." I tried praying and thinking about what I could do next, like I'd always done, but nothing came to mind. I know I went to Gene's grave many times, sometimes at night, but I cannot recall what I did or said there. I think I just sat next to his grave and cried. Sometimes I would hug a nearby oak tree and finally, having spent all my tears, I would leave and go home.

Daddy had taught us a lot of important lessons when we were young. I'll always be grateful to him for telling us that we had to face life as it comes and live it the best you can. Daddy knew this by experience because he'd had his share of disappointments throughout his life. But my problem was that I'd led a relatively pain-free existence up until that moment. Gene's death was my first encounter with the kind of heartache that stops you in your tracks. It was impossible to understand why God let me and Gene's family suffer this way. If someone had told me then that my first experience with that level of pain and grief would not be my last, I might have given up altogether. I could not have handled knowing that there was more to come.

I have since learned that when bad things happen—and they happen to everyone—we have two simple choices. We can either go with the flow or die. Sometimes you can step back, look at your circumstances, and ask yourself, "What's so bad about *this*?" And it may be bad—the worst thing you can imagine—but you cannot let it eat you up.

As hard as it was to go through Gene's death as a young wife and mother, that experience was actually good for me in many ways. For one thing, I learned early on that death is a part of life. Death comes in all shapes and sizes. It may be the death of a loved one, the death of a marriage, or the death of a dream. Some people don't know how much I can relate to people who have gone through all three of those things and more. People don't realize it because I've also had so many blessings in the many lives I've lived.

Without a doubt God was there for me in one of the darkest periods in my life. And He would do it again more than once down the road. A future time was coming when my way grew so dark, so suddenly, that I could not see where to go next. How people get through a crisis without God I do not know.

I'm not saying He was there for me because I've been a perfect person. I'm saying that God has forgiven me, and He has been a refuge for me all the way. I could never be very good. I enjoyed life too much and had a good time, always seeing the funny side to most situations. But I also know that you can be as good as you can be, and it's still not good enough. That's why we need God's grace.

Sometimes people feel as if they're outside of what God wants for them. I understand that because I have felt the same way sometimes. But I believe He hears us when we say, "I'm sorry." Not only that, He's also quick to forgive us. The harder thing is often forgiving ourselves. God doesn't have to do this, you know. We are flesh and blood after all and we'll mess up again. But He is there to forgive us and pull us back to His side when we ask Him to, and it's as if we never left.

No one was ever perfect except for the Lord. Even with all the loving, praying, and serving that we can do, we are still not near what the Lord is. He knows our hearts. He knows how we are, but He loves us anyway. When you are older, you'll find out that it's a good feeling to go to bed at night with the peace that comes from the Lord. You can sleep well thinking of Him and not worrying about tomorrow.

For much of my life, I did not think I would live past the age of seventy for some reason. That seemed old enough to me. Now that I've made it well beyond that, there have been a few good scares and scrapes along the way when I thought that this was truly the end. I've been blessed with good health, but in the past few years

I came very close to dying more than once. What was interesting to me is how I felt during that time. Instead of being terrified of dying, I experienced the sweetest peace I've ever known. God had me by both hands and I knew it.

We have to leave room for God to surprise us. God surprised me by letting me live this long. I'm getting old and it feels good, to be honest. When I somehow managed to put more decades behind me than many of my peers, people began asking me for the secret to aging. I act surprised when they ask and tell them that there's never been a time when I wasn't aging! One gift that age gives you is perspective. Some of the things that we worry about and dread the most, when they finally happen, are not nearly as scary as we thought they might be. When I looked ahead as a young mother facing an uncertain future, I wasn't so sure about that. But then God surprised me.

I HAD NO INTENTION to remarry after Gene died, and I got busy making plans to raise my son as a single mother until my dying day. I needed a job, first of all. But I had never gone to school. Sometimes when I washed up after supper and tucked Richard into bed at night in our new home in Tyler, I would think back to my childhood wish of wanting to become a nurse like Jean. I told Mother about this dream one night when we were up late talking. If I could get my nursing degree, I told her, then I could get a good job and provide some security for Richard.

She thought that was a good idea, so I looked into registering for nursing classes at Tyler Junior College in town. I had just bought all of my supplies, including a stethoscope, scissors, and books, when I got extremely sick the day before school started. A sudden pain in my side was so excruciating that it brought me to my knees. The feeling was all too familiar, and I knew without a doubt what was wrong before the doctor ever told me. I had another severe case of kidney stones.

I would need to have emergency surgery again, followed by a slow recovery, before my life was back to normal. That was the end of the start of my nursing career. Still, God had something else in mind for me. It just wasn't the right time yet for me to know exactly what—or who—that was.

## CHAPTER EIGHT

# A New Start

When my school plans went bust, I made myself take a deep breath and start over. I applied for several jobs in Tyler and waited impatiently for someone to contact me in response. True to my nature, I was ready to get on down the road. I've been that way all of my life. I was always in a hurry to get to the end of one chapter and the start of another throughout my life. When I was a teenager, I wanted to be in my twenties. When I was in my twenties,

I wanted to get going in my thirties. And so on. This
isn't such a bad thing if you have something you can sink
your teeth into waiting around the corner. But if not, I'd
say try not to bite so hard! Wait for the Lord to show
you what He wants you to do. When we're younger, we
really don't need to be in such a hurry to get to the next
phase in life, but sometimes it can't be helped.

While I was on hold for someone to hire me in Tyler,
Richard came through the front door one day with
a terrified look on his face. "Mom," he said, "there are
a lot of policemen outside." My heart sank. It was too
much like the morning when I had seen the couple from
church walking up to my home carrying the worst news
possible. I braced myself and went out the front door to
meet the officers. Was it Daddy? One of my siblings?
To my surprise, I discovered that the police were there
to arrest me! I learned that the nice officer in Ft. Worth
had turned me in for failing to pay a speeding ticket a
year later. After all this time, these policemen were now
at my house to take me to jail for an unpaid ticket that I
never received!

I explained what happened, and though they did not
take me to jail that day, they still said I had to pay. I was
outraged and wanted to fight the charge, but Daddy

came home and talked me into just paying and moving on. Our circumstances were difficult enough, I decided, and I reluctantly let it go. As the months went by with no luck on a job, I was getting more depressed the longer I stayed home. One of Gene's brothers came to visit one day and had a serious talk with me. "Listen," he said, "if you had been taken and Gene was left, he'd be going out and you know it. There's no need to bury yourself here alone. Get out and start meeting people."

I'd felt so guilty for being alive when Gene was gone. But I was only thirty-one years old and God willing had a long life ahead of me. I had to find the strength to go on, at least for Richard's sake.

I finally received a call to work the registration table at a convention, and that eventually led to a full-time job. I began meeting people and going out on a few casual dates. I also started attending a Baptist church in Tyler where a man with the unforgettable name of Finis Fluker was the pastor. Then I began meeting other families and people at church, including one man who held the door open for me and greeted me every Sunday morning.

I had sworn I wasn't going to be interested in anyone, but I found myself taking extra time on Sunday mornings getting my hair just right and picking out the perfect long, flowy dress that was the style back then. I started thinking about this man on my drive to church, wondering if he'd be in his usual spot by the door. Sure enough, he was always there with a big smile on his face. One day after church he asked me out on a date. I knew he was my kind when, instead of going to dinner somewhere, he suggested taking me skiing on Lake Tyler in his boat the next weekend.

First, I liked a man that had his own boat. Second, I was drawn to his adventuresome spirit. I'd never waterskied in my life, but he dared me to try it and that was all it took. I wasn't one to chicken out of anything— especially not a dare—so I agreed to go. The next weekend we got on the water early in the morning. He dragged me all around that lake behind his boat until my arms were limp as noodles and my legs were heavy as lead. But I refused to give in. I tried and tried to get up on my feet on those skis. It was nearly sundown when I finally got on my feet for the first time.

I was so sore that I wished I were dead the day after, but I still had a smile on my face because of the fun we had together. It had been a long time since I'd found someone I was attracted to and even longer since I'd laughed that hard. But he had an easy way about him, and I felt comfortable with him right away.

We began dating, even though I'd sworn off marrying again—especially to a man who was twice divorced and already had three children. After we had been together a while, he confessed that he wasn't an official greeter at church after all. He had seen me one day and carefully planned to be there at the door when I arrived each week just so he could hold it open for me and get to know me!

In time, we grew to love each other very much and started talking about plans for a future together. Robert M. Rogers and I married the next year in 1958.

To my surprise and delight, a special woman from my childhood offered to serve as my wedding coordinator—Mrs. Harmon. She and her husband had moved back to Arp after living in San Antonio all those years. I had the most beautiful wedding and Victorian-themed reception for our family and friends thanks to her. Mrs. Harmon made sure everything was perfect and seemed to consider me one of her own children that day.

MOTHER AND DADDY MOVED out of the little house on Woodhaven and went back to Arp after I got married. Bob moved in with me and Richard, and we became a family. Bob had a young daughter, Sherry, from his first marriage and two small children, Cindy Lou and Robbie, from his second marriage. I loved each one as if I'd given birth to them myself. The children lived with their mothers most of the time, but they came to see us for short visits and stayed longer when they were older.

Cindy Lou was very young when her father and I married. I wanted to be the perfect mom to all of our children, but you know that's not possible. Once when Cindy Lou and Rick were playing in our backyard on Woodhaven, I called them inside for dinner and she was gone. We looked and looked for her and finally called the police. Do you know that they found that little heifer on the Loop and Highway 64 having such a good time that she did not want to go back home?

Sherry and I tell each other often how glad we are that

we are family—and how glad we are that we both like to go shopping! She came into my life at a tender age, and she and Rick became close. I can remember when Sherry joined us on a family trip and she and Rick had to share a bed as young children. Rick was a typical boy and wasn't crazy about sleeping in the same bed with his sister. We split the bed down the middle and told them not to bug each other. We found out later that Rick laid awake suffering for four hours hoping we'd notice that Sherry had accidentally crossed over a little on his side of the bed in the night! I'll never forget when Sherry grew up and went to SMU, she brought home the Kappa Pickers band and we cleared out all the furniture in my den so they could perform. They had it going on! Today Sherry lives in Tyler in a beautiful home, and I see her quite often. When Sherry's husband died, I wanted her to move there and be close by. Of course, I could relate to what she was going through because I had lost a husband, too. (And then I found another one!)

In my family we never refer to one another as "step" this or that. I don't like putting people in categories. We were a family from the start and we stayed that way.

After I gave birth to Richard, Gene and I had talked about having more children. But the doctor told us this was not possible. I was devastated by that revelation and always assumed that it must have been my fault somehow. I loved being a mother more than anything in the world, and it did not make sense to me that God would not want me to have more children.

But Bob and I weren't married six months when I got the shock of my life. I was pregnant with our son Randy! Randy has always been a more reserved person, and he is a very slow boil as far as his temper goes. The story my children love to tell about him was when he was sweeping leaves off our roof outside the kitchen, and I went out to talk to him about what he was doing. He took what I was saying the wrong way and swept the leaves right off the roof and onto my head! I called him down from there and set his world on fire.

Our other two children, Becky and Rusty, soon followed the birth of Randy. In fact, I stayed pregnant the first three years of our marriage. I was one of those rare mothers who enjoyed every minute of pregnancy. All of my babies were born bald and beautiful. In fact, when the nurse told us in the hospital that we'd had a little girl, I did not believe it until I checked my baby's diaper!

When Becky was a child, I dressed her in petticoat

dresses, shined her shoes, and rolled her blonde hair every Saturday night while we watched *The Honeymooners* on television. I thought she looked like Little Miss Sunbeam, but despite my best efforts, she preferred being a tomboy when she was young just like me. I could hardly blame her because that's how I grew up, too.

Even though I'd gone through three days of hard labor with my first child, the next baby was always easier than the last until I finally had a big family like my own. I could not have been more content as a mother in the moments when I had my children around me. They were all the cutest things, of course, and someone would have to be crazy not to love them.

I've seen it happen over and over in life—when what we love goes away, someone or something inevitably comes in to take its place if we'll let it in. Something ends and something else begins.

⁓

WE HAD MANY POSITIVELY good times in our family—whatever we did together was so much fun. At

Christmas, we had a big tree and often invited several other families we knew to share Christmas morning with us while the kids opened gifts. When I was a child, I knew it was Christmastime whenever our home started smelling like fresh fruit. Daddy would buy a bushel of red apples and oranges for our stockings, and their wonderful scent would fill our home, reminding us that something special was happening. The memory of the smell of that fruit basket permeating our home reminds me of a time when that alone was enough Christmas for me.

Like my mother, I wanted to open our home to our friends and family when my children were growing up. My kids knew they were always welcome to bring home friends from church and school. We used to paper houses for fun when the kids were in junior high and high school, throwing rolls of toilet paper over every tree branch, bush, and the mailbox until the entire yard was full of streams of white paper. I could usually be counted on to get more than enough rolls of toilet paper to do a good job. Plus, I loved being the one to drive the getaway car!

One time someone in our church, who also happened to be my cousin, boasted that "nobody would dare" paper his house. "Well," I thought to myself, "I'm going to have to do it." And we did. I don't know how many rolls of paper we used that night. We didn't leave anything in his yard without toilet paper on it by the time we finished. I drove the kids and their friends down the street and we sat on the curb waiting for him to come home just so we could see his reaction! Really and truly, they needed to get papered.

Early in our marriage, Bob and I moved our church membership from the small church where we met to a larger church near us. It was just around the corner from where we'd built a home big enough for our growing family. Green Acres Baptist Church welcomed us and we made many lifelong friends there, especially after Paul W. Powell came to serve as pastor in 1972.

When the kids were older, we built a gymnasium next to our house for parties and get-togethers. My family jokes that it was the first "family life center" long before our church built its own recreation center. I loved it when all the church kids would come over to the gym to play pool, shoot basketballs, and watch television.

I became close with some of my kids' friends this way. I remember looking out the window one weekend and seeing a light on in there well after midnight. I walked over to see what was going on and recognized a young man fast asleep on a couch near the TV. I woke him up and asked, "Does your mother know you are here?" He just grunted. "No, and I'm not talking to her," he announced and turned over. But I had some news for him, and he quickly got up after that and called his mother.

My children became friends with our church friends whose kids were the same age, and we did many things together—including getting in trouble together. My kids papered their friends' houses, ambushed Ken and Bobbie with water guns, and pulled pranks on each other just as I had done when I was young. One Christmas while some of our family friends were at the traditional Christmas Eve service, we staged someone's backyard furniture on the roof of their house like Santa Claus and his sleigh! What a surprise they had when they came home! It didn't take long for them to guess who had done it, and we waited for payback.

When Rick took the trash out one day, he saw a big fat possum by the backdoor. He grabbed it by the tail and taunted some of his siblings with it for a few minutes until a new idea struck. They stuck that poor possum in a gift-wrapped box and left it on the front porch of our friends. But then the phone started ringing with different people telling us the rest of the story of what happened next. Our friends had apparently opened up that box and the possum, they said, had attacked them. One of them had to go to the hospital! Of course, we later learned that this was all a made-up story. When they'd actually opened the box, the possum had done what possums do—it played dead until they could dump it out of the box. They got us back for this trick when we awoke one morning and saw dozens of bags worth of shredded paper covering our yard like snow. We never could clean it all up.

We also spent many an afternoon on Lake Tyler waterskiing with family and friends. By the time my children were young, I had come a long way from the days when Bob took me around the lake all day learning to ski. I had even learned to drive the boat. Whenever I was pulling someone on skis, the kids would beg me to cut the steering wheel hard and sling the skier around to see if they could hang on! I was glad to oblige. We would also go to Lake Tyler's Petroleum Club on long summer days to play during the day and eat dinner as a family when the sun went down.

There are several pictures in our family photo albums

of us fishing together. We went on several fishing trips to Arkansas where we floated the river with a guide. The lake we fished in Sun Valley, Idaho, was so full of fish that every time you threw out a line one bit the hook. But one of our favorite spots to fish was close to home at the lake in Arp. We always dumped our old Christmas trees there every January near our favorite fishing spot to attract more fish and make it easier to get a nibble. When I was a child, we fished with a stick pole and a fistful of bacon. I asked my husband just the other day when we could go fishing this spring after I went to Wal-Mart and discovered that I could get my groceries and my fishing lures at the same store!

Many of my memories of our family and friends took place in Sun Valley where we often took vacations. One time Cathy and Paul Powell came with us on vacation, and the men decided they would hike over two mountains in one day. It was a pretty strenuous hike and they instructed us where to meet them in the late afternoon. Cathy and I made our way to the agreed upon spot when it was time. Only there was one problem. No one was there! We waited and waited, not knowing that the men had taken much longer than they planned to complete the hike. We drove a little further into the forest to look for them, and then they went to the meeting spot and could not find us! It was ages before we finally met up with them again, and by that time we were all so relieved it was hard to be mad at each other.

Sun Valley was also the scene of a snowmobile accident in the 1980s when I crashed head on with another snowmobile. I must have a high tolerance for pain, and I think most women who have had children would say the same thing. I did not think I needed to go to the hospital and kept insisting to everyone that I was perfectly fine. It was not until we were driving home when I started feeling dizzy. My husband rushed me to the hospital only to discover that I'd cracked five ribs and broken my arm. (By the way the man who hit me was not hurt at all.) But I was really broken up and stayed in the hospital for several weeks recuperating. I loved coming home to Tyler in one piece and I was grateful for it. I made sure that I rode the snowmobile again at Spring Break to prove to myself and other people that I was not afraid.

We love sports in our family—especially football, and I am still a raving Dallas Cowboys fan. I once had a parrot named JoJo that I taught to cheer for them. That bird couldn't say a word when I bought him at the pet store, but he learned to mimic my voice and talked up a storm. On command he would hold up his wings and say, "Yippee! Go Cowboys!"

I tried to follow the stars of the Cowboys all around Dallas in the early days. When legends like Roger Staubach and Bob Lily would go out to eat, I'd try to find out where they were so I could be out there waiting for an autograph when they left! My family thought I was crazy.

I went to Super Bowl 30 with Becky and a few of her friends. For the game, I wore dark sunglasses and a blingy jacket in my favorite color blue in honor of my Cowboys. I had gone to the restroom and was walking back to my seat when someone in the hallway pointed to me and said, "Look—there's Troy Aikman's mother." I'm not necessarily an Aikman fan, and I told them that I was not his mom. But they took one look at me and said, "Yah, right." Suddenly there was a crowd beginning to gather around me wanting my autograph! I'm not so sure that it surprised my daughter when I started scribbling "Mom" "Mom" "Mom" on the scraps of paper these Cowboys fans were handing me. I finally got nervous that I was going to get caught and so I just smiled and said, "Y'all, my boy's on the field, and I would just die if I missed him. Gotta go!"

My boys all played softball in Green Acres' church league, and they knew their parents would be in the stands cheering for them at their games. One year we made it to the finals in San Antonio, but the team we were supposed to play to advance into the next round looked tough. Not to mention the fact that they looked as if they were all thirty years old. I thought to myself, "There's no way our boys can beat them." But we did.

I'm afraid I didn't always hold my tongue when I disagreed with a call, but at least I never got thrown out of a game. Which was more than our pastor could say. In the semi-finals in Wichita Falls, I'll never forget when the umpire called a third strike on Paul Powell's son. Paul leapt to his feet and wanted to have a little visit with the umpire about that last call. Back in the stands, all the church members started laughing, anticipating what was going to happen next since Paul was never one to back down. Sure enough, the umpire threw Paul...and his son...out of the game!

When we made it all the way to the state championship, I thought I was going to lose my mind because I was so proud of my boys and our church. At the last out of the game when we knew we were finally going to win, I burst out bawling. I cried like a baby, and some of those boys might even remember that they were crying, too.

∾

I LOVED LIVING IN Tyler and raising a family here. Our home has a circular driveway where, to my family's amusement, I once broke my toe riding my bicycle just to prove that I knew how. I wrecked all over the place, and did you know there's not a thing you can do to help heal a broken toe any faster? We planted fruit trees on the little bit of land around the house and had a small garden. It was our farm away from the family farm in Arp.

Before we built the gym behind the house, we had wild birds and even a horse named Sassy that lived up to her name. The horse was not my doing. Becky wanted to teach Sassy to ride barrels—something that horse had no interest in doing. We even had ducks for a while, but they eventually had to go because they would not stay out of the swimming pool.

In our pasture we also had chicken pens by the dozens.

Rusty fell in love with chickens from the time he was a boy. He spent many an hour researching chicken breeds and going to the Canton trade days to shop for whatever special kind he was interested in at that moment. He raised so many beautiful birds in our backyard—Rhode Island Reds, Silkies, and even some that laid blue eggs. When he left for college, we had to give away all of his birds because he could not take them with him and we weren't going to take care of all of them!

We also raised peacocks for a while, but they got a little out of control. Our two favorite peacocks named Mr. and Ms. P. made their way into our family picture albums, but they were a mess. They are wild animals, you know. I remember hosting a Bible study for several women at my house one day when Mr. P came strutting by the large windows in my living room. He really was a pretty spectacular bird, and he caught the attention of the women. He spread his wings overhead and made sure his beautiful feathers put on quite a show. I was kind of proud of him, then suddenly I realized he was not performing for us but trying to impress Ms. P. who was walking behind him. Before I could get up out of my chair and put a stop to it, they started to mate right before all of our eyes. I ran over and quickly shut the drapes as fast as I could, but the Bible study never could get back on track!

Mr. and Mrs. P came into our lives when my kids saw an ad for peacocks in the paper. It was a farm in the country that could no longer care for their birds because they were frightening the horses. The ad said the buyer could keep as many as you could catch. So Becky and Rusty went there and chased peacocks all day without any luck. Then Rick explained to them that peacocks roost at night just like chickens do. The next evening they went out to that farm and plucked several peacocks out of the trees and took them home. The problems began soon after that. Just like roosters, we quickly learned that peacocks greeted the morning with a loud cry, which they decided to do from their perch right outside our bedroom window. Did you know that a peacock makes sounds like a woman screaming? Those darn birds scared the dickens out of me the first morning I heard them. It was not a sad day when we finally got rid of the last peacock, including Mr. and Mrs. P.

We had a lot of love in our home, but we also believed in disciplining our kids. In my living room, I have a small glass frame holding two pieces of a brown belt with my name carved in the leather. The bronze plaque underneath reads: "The belt that raised four good children." When they deserved a spanking, they got one. But they can't say I pinched their hair like my mother did to me! I spanked my children, but I found out that Bob would sometimes hole up in the bathroom and hit his hand with the belt instead. Then he'd whisper to the kids to yell out as if they were really being punished!

Most important, we taught our children to know Jesus at an early age. I will always treasure the times when each one came to me and said, "Mother, I'm ready." One by one, they walked down the aisle at church and told Brother Paul about their decision to follow Christ. We grew up praying as a family, and we still pray as a family. When each of my children grew up, fell in love and got married, our family grew by one more. When I became a grandparent, we nearly tripped over each other trying to hold those babies in our arms.

IT SEEMS LIKE BAD news comes just when things are going well. Our son Robbie was killed on Mother's Day driving home from Texas Tech University in Lubbock. He was such a precious young man and so much fun. You never knew what he would think of doing next. I can just picture him sitting in his long john underwear out in the deep snow at our place in Vail, reading the newspaper like he was a real businessman. Or the times he and his siblings jumped out of the window into the steaming heated pool right below over and over again. Bob took our young boys to Dallas to see Robbie's body after the accident. He felt it was important to teach them a valuable lesson they would never forget about being careful on the road.

Robbie was buried in Dallas where his mother lived. His dog was also killed in the accident, and they laid his body beside Robbie in the casket. All my boys were so close when they were growing up. Rusty even named his own son after Robbie.

When Cindy Lou and Robbie's mother died outside of Dallas where she lived, it was so sad. Later Cindy Lou told me how she wished her mother and brother were closer so she could visit their graves. So I immediately made plans to move their bodies to a cemetery in Tyler so she could be near her family and visit their graves as often as she liked. I understand the importance of being near your loved ones. I arranged for their bodies to be moved and remember sitting patiently in the graveyard one bittersweet afternoon waiting for the caskets to be delivered and knowing I'd done the right thing for her. Today Cindy Lou lives just outside Tyler and we love to get together for lunch at least once every week so we can laugh and talk together. Her sweet brother Robbie has been gone many years, but he has never left our memory.

⁂

WHEN BOB AND I married, he owned a drive-in theater on Fifth Street in Tyler. We were a good team because he was an entrepreneur at heart—and I was a born risk-taker. We got into the cable business just as cable television was becoming popular. This business became very successful in time. Like anything else worth doing, it required sacrifice, a commitment to hard work, and very long hours—but I was used to all of that because it's the way I grew up.

My favorite teacher in school was a math teacher named Miss Addison. But I always hated math and still do. I don't use it in anything but balancing my checkbook, and I was always good at that. When I realized that our business was doing very well, I knew we would be able to do a lot more for our children—and for others—than I ever could have imagined.

I also felt that God had already blessed us as a family in ways that had nothing to do with money, long before He ever blessed us financially. We would be able to take the kids on wonderful trips and enjoy vacation homes in Vail and Sun Valley as a family—and we did. But most important, I believed we already had more love in our home in Tyler than we could ever hold.

It's not difficult for me to recall the times when I walked over to the Harmon house as a child, sloshing milk out of my bucket and dreaming of the future. "This is just for today. Tomorrow, I will be something else." I'd made myself that promise all of my life, with no earthly reason to believe it would ever come true.

It was a very unlikely dream when you think about it. I grew up in a town of a few hundred people. I never went to college. I happily flipped burgers and was a mother, a widow, a wife, and a business woman. But I never once stopped thinking that I was somehow following some sort of greater destiny—some plan that was bigger than

I was.

Now "tomorrow" was finally here on our doorstep. Life would be different from now on, but it turned out that I'd been wrong about one thing all those years I'd spent dreaming. I had said that one day I would "be something else." But, as it turns out, I was still me. I hadn't changed; only my circumstances took an unexpected turn when God blessed us with a successful business.

I still live in the same house I've lived in for more than sixty years and have many of the same friends I've had all of my life. In my mind, I'm still the girl from Arp, sitting on the front porch with Mother and Daddy shelling peas. It's probably too late to change now anyway.

## CHAPTER NINE

# Blessed to Be a Blessing

"Why don't you go with us?"

Dr. Kerfoot Walker was standing there asking me to join him and a team of people from Green Acres on a mission trip to Belize in Central America. I thought about it for a minute before I answered.

"I'll go," I told him, "if you promise to stay by my side

the whole time." And just like that, I decided to get on a plane and fly into the heart of the jungle.

My friends teased me and said I'd never make it without a hotel or a manicure. But I'd grown up wading in creeks and sleeping under the stars plenty of times. After our mission team departed Houston, we stayed in Belize City the first night in an open area underneath the missionaries' house. When we got up the next day, everyone looked as if they had the measles. The mosquitoes nearly did us in on the very first day, covering us in red bites from head to toe!

We travelled to the airport and piled all our supplies inside an airplane that was smaller than I believed possible. The pilot pointed the nose of that plane toward the jungle where we would live for the week and we took off. When we began our descent after some time, I was looking out the window for any sign of the runway. I saw only a wide patch of grass with a woman waving a red scarf enthusiastically.

We touched down, surrounded by a wild landscape that was a dozen shades of green. I suddenly felt afraid and thought to myself, "What in the world have I done?" All my children were adults by now, but I knew they would not believe it if they knew where their mother was at that moment. And Bob would have gone out of his mind with worry.

After landing, we rode in the back of an old pickup, sitting on uncomfortable wooden planks with splinters digging into our backsides. We finally arrived at a simple gazebo in the middle of a clearing that would serve as our home base. When I signed up for the trip I had imagined being Kerfoot's nurse for the week so I could finally fulfill my lifelong dream. I pictured taking blood pressure, dosing out medicine, and maybe even helping deliver babies or saving someone's life if need be. I waited anxiously as we stood around in a half-circle and Kerfoot gave everyone their assignments. That's when I learned that I was not going to be the nurse after all. Far from it. I was to be the camp cook. It could have been worse, I decided, so I got busy.

For our first meal, one of the local women brought me a rough sack full of dry beans. That's all. When I looked inside, something was moving. Lots of somethings. I peered closer and saw flecks of tiny black weevils crawling throughout the beans. I hesitated and pointed to the bugs, but she just smiled and left me with the sack.

Later, I caught a ride into the nearby village and shopped at an open-air market. There I bought oatmeal, butter, bacon, watermelon, and cantaloupe. I proudly took my bundles of groceries back to camp, thinking through the week's menu and how I was going to do it with limited supplies. The next morning with a little help starting the fire, I cooked a piping hot large pot of oatmeal for our team of eighteen people. I added sugar, butter, a little bacon grease stirred in, and some salt. The villagers who ate with us that morning thought they'd died and gone to heaven! I was back in my element— just like the days at the Toddle House and the Speedway. Each morning I noticed that the breakfast line got a little bit longer because word had spread. But dinner was always the same—beans and rice—although I tried dressing them up as much as possible with what I hand on hand.

I had talked my friend Dixie into going with me on the trip, and I'm sure that we had more fun together than anyone else. I thought Texas was hot, but the jungle was stifling. We would get so hot in the afternoons and went down to the river to cool off every day, even though the minnows would bite the freckles on my legs and make me jump.

It was difficult and dirty work, I don't mind saying. One man decided he couldn't take it after just a few days

in the jungle, and he ended up flying home. We slept
outside under the gazebo with rumpled mosquito nets
draped around our dollar store blow-up mattresses that
weren't even worth a dollar. We also used an outdoor
toilet, which is all I had used growing up so that was not
the worst part for me. When I surprised my friend in the
outhouse in the middle of the night with a flash camera,
she screamed so loud that she woke up the entire camp!
We laughed all the way back to the gazebo and tried our
best to go to sleep without getting into giggle fits.

After three days of working with the villagers, our
leader Kerfoot was covered in dirt, and he did not even
seem to notice. The chocolate candy he carried in his
pocket for the local children had melted into a brown
stream running down his shirt. Dixie and I offered to
wash his clothes in the river when we washed our hair
one day. I'm not sure his shirts came out any cleaner after
the wash, but at least we tried. For dinner that night,
a pastor brought a fistful of crabs with huge pincers
that he'd fished out of that same river where we'd been
bathing! Thinking of those crabs gave me pause the next
day when I went to wash up, and I bathed so fast I broke
a sweat.

The river was also the sight of a beautiful baptism on

our last day when one of the young men on our team decided to become a Christian. We all held hands in the water as Kerfoot baptized him, and it seemed as if the Lord was right there among us.

We flew back to Belize City and then on to Houston to return home at the end of the week. Then it was a long bus ride home back to Tyler. I remember pulling into the church parking lot and seeing Bob running alongside the bus. He was grinning and waving at me to welcome me home as if he had not seen me in weeks. I handed him a nice carved wooden eagle that I'd bought for him. But in the excitement, he dropped it and broke it all to pieces. It didn't matter to me then—I was just glad to be home. When I went to bed that night, I was grateful and treasured the warm feeling I had in my heart from doing something for others.

WHEN I BECAME A Pink Lady, I felt as if I was as close to being a nurse as I would ever be. But surely nurses don't have as much fun as we did! I served many years at

East Texas Medical Center in Tyler in their community volunteer program called the Pink Ladies. On two days of the week we wore pink coats and went room to room to serve coffee and juice to patients. We helped them with whatever they needed, including taking time to pray with them if they asked. I loved volunteering there and considered making people laugh part of the job. Five of my friends were also Pink Ladies, and I volunteered there for close to thirty years. I used to joke that I wanted to be buried in my pink coat because I'd spent so much time in it.

Some people think Christians can't have any fun. That's just not true—you can have all the fun in life that you want. Our adventures as Pink Ladies were legendary. One time I knocked on a patient's door and did not hear a response. I went inside and realized immediately that the patient had died. I calmly walked out as if nothing had happened and called my friend Agnes over.

"He needs some juice," I told her, nodding toward the patient's door. She went in and I waited outside in the hall.

Agnes thought he was just asleep and began asking in a louder and louder voice what kind of juice the poor man wanted until finally the nurse walked in on her. She took one look at the patient and said to Agnes, "Honey, this man has as-pire-ed." Agnes came out of that room ready to kill! But I was already down the hall making my getaway.

I thought I'd had my last encounter with the law when the police showed up in my front yard to arrest me for the outstanding ticket in Ft. Worth. I hadn't counted on being arrested and taken to "jail" at the mall in Tyler decades later. I opened my front door one day and former Sherriff J.B. Smith and another officer stood there holding handcuffs! They were not even smiling. I soon figured out that someone was hosting a fundraiser and this was all part of a game. The sheriff and his men were kidnapping local Tylerites who had to post bail to raise money for charity.

Sylvia, one of my Pink Lady friends, had arranged for me to be picked up on their route. I love a good joke and went along with it, of course. J.B. took me in cuffs to the mall and put me in a fake jail cell alongside other people I knew until I called several of my friends and raised enough money to post my "bail." And I had to raise a *lot* before they'd let me go!

Whoever pulls a joke on a natural born prankster like me had better be prepared for payback. When I found out that Sylvia was behind this scheme, I didn't say a word and even acted as if I had forgotten all about it. I can wait it out a long time when I want to.

One day a few months later, all six of us were eating at the old Fuller's Diner in our pink coats after volunteering at the hospital. Suddenly the sheriff and a news crew burst on the scene. The camera's bright light came on and they filmed the entire thing as the sheriff cuffed Sylvia at the table and hauled her to the real county jail downtown! We threw our heads back and cackled as they drug her out the door, screaming and laughing. It was not one of my best, but it was a good one.

ABOUT THE TIME THAT my time as a Pink Lady was ending, so was my marriage. Bob and I divorced in 1991 when I was sixty-six years old. With every passing year, I can see more of my life from God's perspective. Writing this book has helped me to see that, and I hope to leave these stories and life lessons for my family members who will come after me long after I am gone.

Sometimes you have to look back at life to realize what's going on. When you are in the middle of everything, you're often too close to it to see what God is doing. But He is always up to something. Not everything has to make sense for it to be part of God's plan. But I do believe that everything happens for a reason, and there are no accidents or coincidences. If I had a chance to do everything all over again, I honestly don't think I would do anything different. I do wonder why some things happened to our family, but again, that's part of life. During some of the most difficult times I went through, I learned not to ask, "Why me?" Instead, I thought, "Why *not* me?" Who was I to think that I would not have heartaches?

I did not feel this way about adversity overnight. It takes a long time, many night's sleep missed and lots of "Help me, dear Lord" prayers to get from wherever you are to where God wants you to be. At least that's what it takes for me. And I'm not there yet. Until you get to the end, you're always learning. That's the way to be, if you possibly can.

Some people are easy to correct. I am not and never have been. When I was working in the shipyard, my dad had to travel several hundred miles to Houston and grab me by the arm to get my attention. He knew what was best for me. If I'd dropped out of school like I wanted to do, my life would have turned out so differently. Likewise, I've often needed God to knock me down to get my full attention. I've had so many, many blessings, but I also know what it feels like to be down on the ground. It's better if you can learn what He wants you to learn some other way. But the important thing is to learn it.

I also think it's important to pray—and ask other people to pray for you—during a crisis. I've learned by experience to ask for prayer immediately whenever trouble comes. I went tearing through the woods to the church to get people to pray for my mother when I was a child. When Gene died, I prayed harder still. Then when I learned that my marriage of thirty-four years was suddenly over, I did not miss a beat. I went to church the next day and asked my Sunday school to pray for me so that I could stay on the road. It may be very difficult and humbling to ask for prayer when you need it. But when I asked, the Lord kept me close.

Why doesn't life turn out the way we planned? I believe that's when God is testing us. We learn about ourselves and what we're made of even long after the test is over. And God will usually work at both ends of the matter to get you back on track because He loves us that much. Life is like a beautiful orchard and sometimes we march in there and chop it all down. It's so painful and we're left with a mess of our own making. It takes years to grow back and it often never does.

I no longer waste time worrying about why bad things happen. I've finally realized that there are far more good things that outweigh the bad. And, as has sometimes been the case in my life, good can come as a direct result of the bad.

THOSE WHO KNOW ME well know that without a doubt I really believe in love and in having the deepest kind of love for family and friends, for God, and for my church. I believe in love because I've had it, and I don't regret any of it. I've experienced it in every way possible. My best advice to anyone is to love the people you love with all your heart and tell them how much you love them often. That's what I most want people to remember about me—that I loved life and I loved people. A good laugh with someone you love is worth more than a million dollars.

I hadn't planned on remarrying after my divorce. Then I met a man who was also a great dancer and he swept me off my feet. But that's another story.

## CHAPTER TEN

# The Best Is Yet to Come

I had no intention of staying down in the dumps after my divorce. I could have stayed home, but I'm not that kind of person. Don't get me wrong. I grieved when I got divorced—I mean, face down on the floor grieving—but somehow my heart did not break. Looking back, it seems like the Lord protected my heart that way and gave me plenty of people to love and support me throughout that time.

When we were going through the divorce, my son Rick had an interesting experience. He told me that he was shaving one morning and suddenly imagined my face next to his in the bathroom mirror. He felt as though he could see me crying and needing help, so he got in the car and drove over to the house to check on me. I was living alone at the time, and that morning I had been face down on the floor crying so hard that my face hurt. My son came in the door calling my name. When he found me, he gently got down on the floor with me, scooped me up, and held me in his arms for two hours to let me cry it all out. I didn't really cry anymore after that day. I was finished.

Some people have God in their life and yet stay defeated. Not me. One of the things I did after the divorce was to get busy. I had stayed home for the first year after Gene's death, and I did not want to do that again. Instead I threw all my energy into becoming very active in our community. I focused on a small college in Marshall, Texas, called East Texas Baptist University. They asked me to serve on their board of trustees, which required me to drive over to their campus for meetings periodically. I made the hour-long drive on the winding countryside roads and spent much of that time alone talking with the Lord. I love going for long drives in the country, and I look back on those quiet moments as one of the ways God helped heal me.

I remember going to Marshall for a football game one afternoon in the midst of a Texas heatwave. We were all sweltering in the stands under the hot sun, not to mention the boys on the field who were wearing all their pads. Finally, I turned and asked one of the school leaders why in the world they were playing ball in the middle of the day instead of later in the evening when it was dark.

"Well, ma'am, we don't have any lights to play at night," he explained matter-of-factly.

"Well, let me help you get some lights!" I said and wiped my brow. It seemed simple enough to me.

Soon after that day, we all had a great time watching those ETBU Tigers play their football games in a lighted stadium under the night sky when it was not nearly as hot!

JOSEPH Z. ORNELAS AND I have been married over
twenty-five years now. He has become so precious to
me over the years. I think it's perfect that we met in a
dance studio because dancing has always meant so much
to me since the time I was a young girl. After we later
married in 1992, we had the time of our lives traveling
and staying active in East Texas. I also kept busy trying
to do what God wanted done with what He gave me.

When I was milking cows as a child I'd often think
about how if I had money I'd be the happiest person in
the world. I've since learned that this is not true. People
think they are buying things without realizing that those
things can soon own them. When we made money in
business, I was happy for a while buying material things.
But I also remembered a lesson from the Harmons. I'd
desperately wanted what the Harmons had all of my
childhood. The money, land, house—everything. Then
when I was older I saw that even with all that money you
could still be unsteady on your feet. When I thought

of all the troubles people had despite their money, I thought to myself, "I don't want *that*." The Harmons' son often came to our home when he was grown up, and I never could figure out why he did that when he had that beautiful house on the hill. It perplexed me until I understood that our little house in Arp, as simple as it was, was full of love. No amount of money could buy that.

Money never made anyone happy, and it does not necessarily make me happy either. Giving it away does. God made us a certain way so that sometimes when we finally get what we think we want most in life, we find out that we don't really want it after all. I don't know why He made us that way, but it's a good way to make us.

I grew up during the Great Depression, and my parents were always more concerned with other people than with their own needs. Daddy especially was a stickler for giving to others. We sometimes did without so that my parents could have more to help those who were barely getting by. One time Daddy lined the floor of our barn with heavy paper for a family to stay there several days. Mother brought them her flour to cook with and shared some of her potatoes and other vegetables from our garden.

I like to think that I'm somehow following in their footsteps whenever I'm able to help someone else. I'm thankful for the opportunities we've had over the years to help, and that includes doing special things for my own parents. I've always had a thing for cars, so as soon as I could do it, I bought my mother the car of her dreams. I surprised her with a beautiful new Cadillac waiting in the parking lot when we left her favorite restaurant one night. The dealership put a big red bow on top, and she cried when she saw it, she was so happy. I also wanted to give Daddy one, but I never got the chance before he died.

Education is one of my favorite causes to support. Some of the buildings I've been able to help construct are named in honor of the name my father gave my family—Herrington. I'm especially pleased that his name is on the campus of the University of Texas at Tyler and Baylor University because he valued education, even if he never received a degree himself. Tyler Junior College was even kind enough to award me an honorary Nursing degree in 2000 over fifty years after I registered for classes!

I much prefer to give money away to good causes and good people. I don't care about getting anything. These days there's nothing I need, nothing I want. But I also splurge on myself occasionally. One of my early splurges was a white Excalibur car with horns on the fenders and white sidewalls. That sounds like a Texan, doesn't it? It was awesome, but it was also the kind of car that you just had to drive fast. I've only received one speeding ticket in my whole life. Two, if you count the one in Fort Worth. I was coming home to Tyler late one night from visiting Mother in Arp. I had just crossed Mud Creek, the darkest part of that highway, when all my childhood fears of being in the woods at night got the best of me. I started hurrying to get through it when a police officer turned on his flashing lights behind me.

I went to drivers school to remove the speeding ticket from my record, and I learned so much that day that I almost enjoyed it. They did not teach us much when I got my license as a teenager. The first time I drove a car was in Daddy's pickup behind our house. I was only fourteen years old and his truck was parked in the pasture near a wood pile. That truck said, "Come get me, Lou." So I did. I would have gotten away with it too, except the pickup got stuck when I accidentally ran over the pile of wood! I had to go get Daddy and tell him what I'd done this time.

When my father died on October 17, 1980, the hole he left in our hearts was so great that our family would never be the same. He was born in 1897 and had lived a long time, although it would never have been long enough for those of us who loved him. My father farmed his land and grew something on it until the time he got sick and could no longer work at it. I remember wanting to help him one day when I was visiting them from Tyler. He had a pile of potato vine clippings that he wanted to plant. You don't have to have roots or a potato to grow potato vines—just a clipping will do. I carefully placed each one and tamped it down with my foot into the soil. I thought I'd done a good job until I looked and saw Daddy was coming behind me, fixing each one just the way he wanted it done. He always had a certain way he wanted to do things.

Daddy was in good health until the very end. He knew it was bad by the time he was in a hospital bed in Tyler—even though the doctors told him that he'd rally right up to the day he died. They told us to go home from the hospital and assured us that Daddy would be back to working in his garden in no time. I smiled at Daddy, kissed his face, and told him I would see him the next day.

But something in my heart told me that was not true. I had seen how sick he was. Daddy had tried to hide his pain from us, like he did all the times when Grandfather Haire put Daddy in his place. This time the pain was too great for my father to keep to himself, and we knew the time was drawing near.

Mother was so tired, trying to be at the hospital for him while fretting over her children and making sure we were all doing okay. We went home as the doctors suggested, but then we went right back to Daddy's hospital room a few hours later. My father died that afternoon surrounded by his family.

BY NOW I'VE OUTLIVED all but two of my siblings and nearly all of my childhood friends. My younger brother Al died at the age of 89 while I was writing this book. I have so many memories of him because we were so close in age.

I'll never forget how dapper he looked all dressed up for a date one night when we were growing up in Arp. Al was whistling and singing the entire time he was getting ready. When he went out the door with his hat cocked on one side of his head like he was really something, Jean and I just looked at each other. It wasn't long before we had hatched a plan to take our brother down a notch. She drove me to town where my brother and his date were eating at a small café. As Jean and I had rehearsed, I burst in on my brother pretending to be his wife! I even slapped him across the face and told him he better come home right then and help me with the baby. His date just sat there wide-eyed while he pleaded with her to stay and swore up and down that I was his sister! I thought I did a masterful job. Al, however, did not think it was so funny. He chased me out the door of the café as I ran to the car, and I'm sure he wanted to kill us both. Jean and I laughed all the way home.

The last time I saw Al in the hospital before he died, we held hands and the blood flowed between us as only family can do. He was my brother, and more important, he was my lifelong friend. Sometimes I still cannot believe that he's gone.

When someone you love dies, it doesn't matter how many funerals you've been to before—it is just as painful as the very first one. But the pain that comes with grief is something like a hammer. The initial blow when a loved one dies hurts so much, but with time the pain grows lighter and lighter.

When I look back on my life, I can see God was at work the whole time. If I'd never lost Gene, I probably would have lived in West Texas most of my life. I may not have moved back to Tyler to be near family. And if I had not done that, I would not have been able to help as many people and organizations as I've had the privilege to help over the years.

It hurts me most of all to think that I wouldn't have had more children. I believed what the doctor told me about not being able to have kids, but the doctor was wrong. Many times in my life people have told me "that will never happen," and I always tend to think, "By George, it will too." Sometimes other people want to keep you down, and they don't really believe you or anyone can do it. They may have been taught to think that way, but their negative example is there for you to see and choose which way you want to be. I grew up believing that I can do it if I try hard enough. And if the Lord helps me with it, then we certainly could do it.

The fact that God blessed me with several children is one of the reasons why I consider having a houseful of people who mean the world to me one of life's greatest pleasures. Dick Sulser worked for us many years ago starting at the First National Bank in Whitehouse in 1983 and has been my assistant since that time. We've shared a lot of laughter and a lot of tears. He calls me Gladys and I jokingly call him Leroy. I'm also grateful to Denise Grubbs who came into our lives. She has been a wonderful help to us. Spending time with family and friends is the most important part of any day. To me, family is everybody that's around you. They're all family. I recently celebrated my 92$^{nd}$ birthday with a family Wahoo tournament with prizes and matching red t-shirts for everyone. The oldest to the youngest turned out for the occasion, and I even got to hold my great-grandbaby. We can get very competitive in our family, and I went "out" in one of the early rounds!

Even though all my children are grown and I've been retired many years, I sometimes feel busier than I've ever been. I meet with various people, attend events when I can and keep up with paperwork and correspondence. But I can also appreciate a good meal at Cotton Patch Café during the week with friends and a Doris Day movie on a rainy day on the Turner Classic Movies channel.

If I'm ever faced with choosing Humphrey Bogart or Clark Gable, anyone who knows me will tell you that Clark Gable would win every time. I liked Bogart's movies, but I never cared much for him because he looked to me like somebody who dipped snuff! When my grandparents from Mississippi visited us as kids, those days were heavenly, except for the time some of us became sick after we got into Grandmother's snuff bottle. We'd never had any of that around our house. But we found her bottle and had no sooner shoved in a mouthful of that awful stuff when Daddy walked in. He pretended not to see it and made us go with him outside to pick up trash. We held it in our mouths for as long as we could stand it until we finally blew up and spit it all out. It's a wonder Daddy did not make us swallow it to teach us a lesson. Jesus is the Great Teacher, you know, and His lessons stick with us far longer than anything our parents can teach us.

People often ask me what my secret is for living this long, but it doesn't seem that long to me. I often tell people what my Mother and Daddy taught me—that hard work is good for you. I've worked hard all my life, and I know that I would rather work for something than have it handed to me. I've also taken good care of myself, and there is a lot to that, if you want to live a long time. I used to smoke when I was younger until one of my kids found my hidden pack of cigarettes, wet them, and put them back. I quit cold turkey one day and never looked back. I don't have a lot of vices, but I do like a warm slice of banana bread and could eat my favorite chicken salad every day of my life.

Most of all, if you want to live a good life, you must have the Lord by the hand. He holds my hand all the time. Even though I thought I would die much earlier, I am glad God gave me extra years with my family and friends. My mother lived to the age of 104 in the home I bought for her for many years. I enjoyed going over to her house for a cup of coffee on the spur of the moment, and I cherish the times we could just sit and talk. I was a grown woman, but I needed her still and it meant so much to have her close by.

She was in the hospital about a week before she died. I could tell she was going down fast, and she moved to hospice care at the end. The doctor came in her room on April 13, 2007 and told us that we better prepare to let her go. I told her sweet things and stroked her hand. I was beside myself knowing that Mother was about to die, and she would never hug me or kiss me again. Her children did not leave her side for a moment, we were all so crazy about her. I could barely bear to leave her body after she was gone.

I DON'T KNOW IF I will make it to 104 years of age like Mother, but I've lived a good while. More important, I'm content in the Lord—whatever He has for me is alright with me. Whenever I run into a challenge, and they come every day at this age, I tell myself, "I'm not down and out yet, so I'm going on." And I do.

What I enjoy the most about life these days are the same things I've always treasured since I was young: my faith, my family and my friends. The best part of having a big family like mine is loving so many people— and having so many who love you back. I adore all my children, grandchildren, and great-grandchildren. I've always tried to make sure they know that, and I'd like to be around to watch them live their lives for as long as possible.

I also plan to keep all one hundred acres of the old

Harmon place in Arp in the family. After all, that's where this whole story began. When I get to the last chapter one day, it really won't be over. I believe the story of the girl from Arp is just beginning, and the best is yet to come.